EVEN IN THE DARKEST HOUR

LAMENT AS A PATH TO GOD

MICHAEL HUSTON

DESERET BOOK
SALT LAKE CITY

*This book is dedicated to my wife:
Without your loving support and encouragement
it would not have been possible.*

*A special thanks to Eric Lacey, my children, and Celia Barnes,
who all played an important role in bringing this to fruition.*

© 2024 Michael D. Huston

All rights reserved. No part of this book may be reproduced in any form or by any means without permission in writing from the publisher, Deseret Book Company, at permissions@deseretbook.com. This work is not an official publication of The Church of Jesus Christ of Latter-day Saints. The views expressed herein are the responsibility of the author and do not necessarily represent the position of the Church or of Deseret Book Company.

DESERET BOOK is a registered trademark of Deseret Book Company.

Visit us at deseretbook.com

Library of Congress Cataloging-in-Publication Data

(CIP data on file)
ISBN 978-1-63993-240-5

Printed in the United States of America
PubLitho, Draper, UT

10 9 8 7 6 5 4 3 2 1

CONTENTS

Introduction 1
1. Joy and Misery 7
2. Sadness Acknowledged 14
   A Brief Diversion on the Genre of Lament 32
3. Worshipping through Lament 42
4. Finding Our Voice through Lament 54
5. Using Lament to Hold On 74
6. Communal Lament 81
   A Brief Diversion on What Lament
      Might Look Like 91
   Theodicy 106
7. Finding Newness (Eventually) 110
   A Brief Word on Lament and "Faith Crisis" 139
   Notes 143
   Bibliography 152

INTRODUCTION

I have always struggled with sadness and grief, but not in the ways one might expect. Though mental illness has made appearances in my family tree, I have largely avoided the bouts of clinical depression and anxiety with which some of my close family, friends, and associates have suffered. By nature, I am somewhat optimistic and tend to believe (almost to the point of naivete) that things can and will be better than they are now. Further, I tend to believe (almost to the point of pride) that if I "just do [fill in the blank]," then whatever is bothering me will go away. These predilections of personality were reinforced in my formative years: I grew up a member of the Latter-day Saint community in a white, middle-class home in suburban America. I was steeped in the positive-mindset mentality, with the belief that faithful dedication and commitment could overcome almost any challenge. I don't say this to disparage, in any way, my upbringing; this was just the way it was for everyone I knew. Whether it was triumph on the soccer pitch, good grades in school, or success on a mission, the answer to almost any problem was deepened commitment, firmer faith, and harder work. In short, I believed in a straightforward approach to life: commitment + faith + hard work = success/happiness/joy.

Implicit in this worldview is the belief that sadness and grief could largely be avoided by faithfully taking the right steps, in the right order, at the right time. Thus, my struggle with sadness and grief centered around the view that I should be able to *avoid* feeling sadness and grief. So, when sadness and grief came—and they did—I harbored a sense of shame for these feelings, since, as it seemed to me at the time, these feelings were an indication that I lacked commitment, faith, or work ethic. In order to compensate, I buried the sadness, grief, and shame as deeply as possible and quietly tried to figure out what I needed to fix so these feelings could go away.

Though I could point to many times in my life when this approach proved to be more problematic than helpful, one particular moment comes to mind. I had been on a mission for a little over a year. I was serving in Northern Utah and had been in the same area for a few months. The area covered only three wards—which in Utah was about nine square blocks. I had, quite literally, knocked on every single door in my area at least two times. I had personally spoken to nearly everyone, and I knew the life stories of most of the people in the area. It was around my second Christmas away from home, it was cold and snowy, and daylight was in short supply. We had no one to teach, with no prospects of new investigators on the horizon. I had a brand-new companion, fresh out of the MTC, who was homesick and needed emotional support. I was overwhelmed and exhausted. I felt unsuccessful and emotionally drained. All this culminated in a foreboding sense that my relationship with God was on shaky ground.

Things came to a head one day when my companion and I were walking down the road knocking on the same doors I had knocked on multiple times before (that day, more than one person exclaimed, "You again? I already told you I wasn't interested!"). I was the senior companion and the district leader, and I felt responsible for the salvation of the people in my area, but I had nothing left to give and I felt distant from God. I could feel the sadness and grief settle into my bones like frost on a winter night. So, I did what I had always done: I buried the sadness and grief down deep (and the shame even deeper) and resolved to push myself harder—I had to fix what was wrong so that we could find someone to teach and get back into a good spot with God. Resolve (or maybe desperation) washed over me. I walked so quickly between houses that my companion had to jog to keep up with me. I tried to speak with extra conviction when someone opened the door. I even considered going to a Japanese-speaking family's house and trying to speak Japanese (which I most definitely do not speak, but maybe the gift of tongues would kick in?) to show God that I was willing to try everything. My companion raised concerns, but I would not listen because I had to work my way out of this rut and back into a relationship with God. In my mind, I thought, *blessings come to those who are committed, work hard, have faith, and do what God says, and so the solution for sadness and grief is to be more committed, work harder, and be more obedient. And that is exactly what I am going to do.* For weeks and weeks, we followed the missionary handbook with zealous exactness and worked frenetically.

It will probably come as no surprise that these somewhat manic efforts did not lead to a change in my situation. The sadness and grief I felt did not go away, nor did the shame that accompanied those feelings. I continued to struggle to feel God's presence. In fact, rather than things getting better, they got worse for me and for my companion—or to be clearer, *I made things worse for me and my companion.* In my drive to assume responsibility for "fixing" whatever it was that was causing me to feel sadness and grief (since, I thought, the sadness and grief were a result of my not doing something right in the first instance), I was driving our companionship into the ground. Change did eventually come, but not in the way that might be expected.

What finally got us back on the right track was my companion's homesickness. Or more accurately, my companion's expression of his homesickness. One day, he broke down. He finally said what he was feeling, which was something along the lines of: I just can't do it anymore. Why isn't God helping? We're doing everything we're supposed to do. We're working to the point of exhaustion. I miss my family. I believe God can make things better, but where is God now? Maybe I should just go home. My companion was open and honest in expressing his sadness and grief. His emotions were raw but authentic. There was a deep sincerity about what he said that was palpable. His language was not vindictive or abusive; rather, his was a voice of mourning and hurt, *and* of faith. I finally listened, and we talked for a long time. Though I was too insecure in my own emotional development to be as honest and authentic as he had been, he had said what needed to be said and he had been heard by God, and somewhere deep inside I think we both knew it. In the end, my companion decided not to go home, and we served together for a few months. He ended up being one of my favorite companions. I still think of him fondly. Our situation in that area never really changed, but *we* changed. We felt a sense of newness and freedom that was unexpected and remarkable. We were closer to each other and closer to God.

I realize that this story may not seem immediately applicable to some. What matters here, and the reason I began with this story, is not the specific situation (i.e., being on a mission) but to share a time in my life when I felt completely overwhelmed as I carried the heavy weight of sadness and grief that would not go away. What is important in this story is not necessarily how I struggled at a certain point on my mission but the fact that I felt distant from God and that I had no idea what to do about it except work harder and bury the shame I felt. Whether one served a mission or not, I believe that everyone has had times in their lives when those feelings have come—that is part of the human experience—and many of us are not well equipped to understand how those moments fit into our worship practices (I certainly was not). Looking back on this experience, I now see an important key to holding on to covenant relationships in the midst of these hard feelings. And that is what I hope to explore in this book.

There are three overarching themes that I will explore in the chapters that follow. First, though the specifics may vary, my sense is that many people can relate to the worldview I described above. For many of us, faith and hard work are often seen as the keys to overcoming most challenges. We just need to follow the now-apocryphal aphorism, "Pray as though everything depends on God and then work as though everything depends on you." This guidance is not only common in Church life, but this guidance is also seemingly embedded in all aspects of life: work, home, family, etc. We all just need to "put our shoulder to the wheel" and success will come. This approach to life, encapsulated in the image of the beehive, is not inherently wrong and in fact has been a cornerstone of the Latter-day Saint community's survival. Yet, as I learned on a mission, there will *also* be times in our life where challenges and hardships come due to no fault of our own—sometimes life is just hard and stays that way—and there may not be anything we can really do about it. What does it look like to stay in a covenant relationship with God during these times when more commitment, more faith, and more work do not seem to make things better?

Second, it is my experience that the approach to God that is most common in Latter-day Saint and other Christian church services, meetings, or sanctioned gatherings is often praise-focused. It is an approach that centers on the good that God does and the blessings we receive because of Jesus Christ's gospel. It fosters the type of language that always ends with an exclamation point. As a missionary, because my approach to God was nested within a praise-focused framework, I did not know how to maintain a relationship with God when my soul was burdened with sadness and grief. What does one say when one cannot express praise? How does one maintain connection to God from *within* our pain?

Third, building the kind of durable relationships for which we are aiming—namely, eternal companionship with our friends, family, loved ones, and God—is foundationally premised on complete authenticity. This authenticity requires that all of our life's experiences be woven into the cloth of these relationships. Being selective about the kinds of emotions we share with those we love inhibits true connection. But how do we foster an authentic relationship with God when such authenticity could lead us to expressing frustration or even anger about our situation? Is it even possible to faithfully express those feelings to God?

I have come to believe that lament offers us a path to address all three points above. *Lament* is faithfully taking complaints to God. It is how we worship from *within* our pain. To be clear, lament is only one part of our worship, and maybe only a small part. But without lament, our worship and our relationships with those we love can never be complete. When I finally internalized what this meant, it evoked a mix of surprise and deep relief. Lament meant that my grief and sadness could be used as a vehicle for *greater connection* with God, not as a thing that I had to overcome before I could approach God. Lament gave me a way to embrace more of myself and to commit more of myself to God. Lament helped me see that God embraces every part of who I am. This realization felt like exhaling a breath I had been holding for many decades. Lament helped make me feel more whole.

But lament is *more* than just a deeper embrace of who we are (as if that is not enough). Lament has the power to transform us, our families, and our communities. Lament can motivate action, anticipates deliverance, and opens the possibility for newness in our lives. I believe that if, as a young missionary, I had understood the important role of lament as an aspect of my personal worship and a way to deepen my relationship with God in times of hardship, I would have been more open to the newness that God was preparing for me. The same holds true for the small worship community that was my two-person companionship; better equipped to understand the power of lament, we would have been better able to love those we served, who were also in the midst of life's storms. I am slow to learn life's lessons, so I make no claim at perfecting this gospel principle (or any gospel principle for that matter). However, I have come to appreciate the power of lament and hope that this small offering will bring greater wholeness, deliverance, and newness in all the spaces where these are needed.

CHAPTER 1

JOY AND MISERY

WE ARE HAPPY...

Happiness and joy are a core part of Latter-day Saint identity. It is who we are. And why would we not be happy and joyful? If it is the case that "wickedness never was happiness" (Alma 41:10), then a simple inversion of the statement suggests that "righteousness always will be happiness." Those who have embraced and strive to live the restored gospel of Jesus Christ—which helps us access the Atonement of Jesus Christ through the truths, principles, and ordinances it brings to us—should be among the happiest and most joyful people on earth. The plan by our heavenly parents presented to us in the premortal existence is called, among other things, "the great plan of happiness" (Alma 42:8).

Studies on the subject seem to support the notion that Latter-day Saints are a happy people. A recent study by the Pew Research Center suggests that individuals who are actively religious tend to describe themselves as happier.[1] When taken alongside other Pew Research Center data that point to members of The Church of Jesus Christ of Latter-day Saints participating in religious services at the second highest rate of the faith traditions surveyed (that is, they are actively religious), it is easy to see why nearly 81 percent of members reported feelings of "peace and spiritual well-being" weekly.[2] In fact, at the time this was printed, Utah ranked in the top ten among all U.S. states[3] for community well-being, according to the Community Well-Being Index.⁴ As a general rule, it seems, Latter-day Saints are indeed joyful.

Among previous Church Presidents, Gordon B. Hinckley, President of the Church from 1995 to 2008, may be remembered best for his emphasis on happiness. He regularly encouraged Latter-day Saints to cultivate positivity, even when facing life's challenges. In *Teachings of Presidents of the Church: Gordon B. Hinckley*, there is an entire chapter focused on this aspect of his prophetic ministry.⁵ Emblematic of President Hinckley's teaching on the subject is the aphorism that has found its way onto the walls of many Latter-day Saint homes: "In all of living have much fun and laughter. Life is to be enjoyed, not just endured."⁶

But President Hinckley is not the only, or even the most recent, prophet to voice this principle. In a general conference address while he was still the President of the Quorum of the Twelve Apostles, President Russell M. Nelson stated, "When the focus of our lives is on God's plan of salvation . . . and Jesus Christ and His gospel, we can feel joy regardless of what is happening—or not happening—in our lives." President Nelson explained that "Saints can be happy under every circumstance. . . . The joy we feel has little to do with the circumstances of our lives and everything to do with the focus of our lives."⁷ Since becoming President of the Church, President Nelson has continued to teach this concept, and it is a theme that has been picked up and repeated numerous times. But Presidents Joseph Smith, Gordon B. Hinckley, and Russell M. Nelson are only three among the expansive chorus of Church leadership voices that have taught variations of this same basic message: happiness and joy are part of God's plan and something we can feel anywhere and at any time.

. . . BUT SOMETIMES WE ARE SAD

Except sometimes, even members of the Church of Jesus Christ are neither happy nor joyful.

While happiness and joy are possibilities in this life, the fact remains that sometimes, despite our best efforts to choose happiness and to be joyful, and regardless of how obedient we are and how focused we are on Jesus, there will be days in our lives—for some people, many, many days—where neither happiness nor joy come easily or quickly. Recent statistics from Utah, which has a high concentration of Latter-day Saints, indicate that members are not immune to these struggles. A 2021 story in the Church-owned *Church News* discusses research that shows that "Utah does, in fact, have a higher adolescent suicide rate than the national average. . . . Suicide is the second leading cause of death for ages 10–17 in the state and Utah has the fifth highest rates in the nation. Roughly 40% of suicide deaths in Utah were identified as involved—either them or a parent—with the Church."[8] And, according to the Centers for Disease Control and Prevention, around 30 to 40 percent of adults in Utah report symptoms of anxiety or depression.[9] Latter-day Saints may be a happy people generally, but we are not exempt from life's challenges, nor are we free from the sorrow and grief that accompany those challenges.

Recently, some aspects of this reality have been more openly acknowledged. Elder Jeffrey R. Holland's October 2013 general conference address, "Like a Broken Vessel," was a watershed moment in opening the dialogue about and taking steps to destigmatize depression within the Church. Five years later, Jane Clayson Johnson's book *Silent Souls Weeping* continued the conversation.[10] And in the October 2019 general conference, Sister Reyna I. Aburto of the Relief Society General Presidency revisited the topic again in her address "Thru Cloud and Sunshine, Lord, Abide with Me!" With this solid foundation, discussions about depression and other forms of mental illness will likely continue to occur in general conference, on podcasts, and in homes worldwide.

We are a better people for being open and honest about the reality of mental illness and the impact it has on individuals, families, and communities. It is a reality faced by many faithful members and their loved ones. These conversations need to continue, because mental illness likely impacts all of us to some degree or another. Barbara Brown Taylor astutely observes, "Anyone on a spiritual path needs help from time to time in telling the difference between divine disturbance and mental disorder."[11] That can be especially true in times of sorrow, despair, loss, and grief.

All of us need help from time to time, and more help is always better than less help. So, in addition to whatever steps individuals are taking on their own or with the support of their loved ones, if mental illness is present in *your* life or the lives of *your* loved ones, Elder Holland's counsel should be carefully considered: "Seek the advice of reputable people with certified training, professional skills, and good values. Be honest with them about your history and your struggles. Prayerfully and responsibly consider the counsel they give and the solutions they prescribe. If you had appendicitis, God would expect you to seek a priesthood blessing *and* get the best medical care available. So too with emotional disorders. Our Father in Heaven expects us to use *all* of the marvelous gifts He has provided in this glorious dispensation."[12] Though this book may be helpful for those with mental illness (diagnosed or undiagnosed), it is not intended to take the place of appropriate professional intervention.

While mental illness can impact our happiness and joy, it is equally true that even when mental illness is not part of the equation, the human experience still contains suffering and sorrow. Everyone, including those without any mental illness—whether for a short time or for years at a time—will likely experience periods of unrelenting, blinding, backbreaking sorrow, sadness, and misery. Loss, disaster, tragedy—life is filled with it. And just as it is the case that the sun rises on the evil and the good (see Matthew 5:45)—that is to say, everyone—it is equally true that bad things happen to good people (see

Romans 5:2–5; James 1:2–3). Elder Robert D. Hales put it bluntly: "Suffering is universal."[13]

It is tempting to attribute the sadness and misery that accompany loss, disaster, and tragedy to bad actions on the part of the person suffering.[14] Perhaps this is true sometimes; we humans have a proclivity for putting ourselves in bad situations. But this is not the case all of the time. Though this view might make our moral math work (bad actions = suffering), the view that all sadness and misery are the result of the suffering person's actions may also result in our not feeling any responsibility to identify with that individual or help ease that suffering—after all, they did it to themselves. It is similarly tempting to attribute all of life's challenges, no matter how severe, to part of a heavenly test administered in every detail by God, leading to the idea that people should see all of life's challenges as guided by divine intent. I am not discounting this in full, but again it seems unlikely to me that this is the case most of the time. Moreover, while it may help the universe feel more ordered for some, this view invokes age-old questions about theodicy (discussed later)—the justice of God—that are even more challenging: How could a good and loving God be responsible for all of the terrible things that have occurred, are occurring, and will occur? Sourcing all grief to God could also be used as a reason to avoid helping those in pain (after all, if God caused it, who are we to intervene?). In sum, both approaches—blaming the victim or attributing all suffering to God—are attempts to makes sense of the hardest part of our lives. It can be hard—even scary—to stare at the stark reality of the pain we and others experience. But the fact is that whatever the causes, alongside joy and happiness, the human experience can be riddled with pain, even for faithful, obedient Latter-day Saints.

SORROW AND GRIEF ARE PART OF LIFE

My point here is not to rain on anyone's parade. Rather, I want to acknowledge humbly that sometimes parades get rained out.

Sometimes the rain is hard and brief; sometimes the rain is light but persistent; sometimes the rain is a monsoon that never seems to stop. No matter how carefully we plan or how diligent our preparation is, where there are parades there will also inevitably be rain from time to time. Loss, disaster, and tragedy vary in scale, intensity, and duration, but they also occur in the life of every human. And when this reality comes into *our own lives*, to continue the parade/rain analogy (perhaps too far), being thankful for the rain is sometimes not enough to ease the sadness that accompanies the loss of a canceled parade. And sometimes the rain is so strong and lasts so long that it washes away our hope that there will ever be another parade.

Walter Brueggemann, a Hebrew Bible scholar whose work on lament helped change the course of scholarly discourse surrounding this topic, discusses this reality with precision and insight. He says that life is "savagely marked by disequilibrium, incoherence, and unrelieved asymmetry. In our time—perhaps in any time—that needs no argument or documentation."[15] In his classic novel *The Princess Bride*, William Goldman uses humor to express the same idea just as directly: "Life is pain. . . . Anybody that says different is selling something."[16] And in the television show *The Good Place*, Eleanor Shellstrop (played by Kristen Bell) explains to a friend that humans are "all a little bit sad, all the time. That's just the deal."[17] Even with a plan of happiness, it is simply a fact that happiness and joy will be elusive at times, in all of our lives.

Honestly accepting this hard reality is not a denial of faith. In fact, accepting this reality is the *beginning* place for a more open and honest covenant relationship with God. But accepting this reality may also lead us to ask some hard questions. Why am I suffering? What does it mean for my faith when sadness, sorrow, and misery come (and stay)? What am I to do when the experience of life's loss, disaster, and tragedy calls my faith into question? How can I relate to God when, in my own lived experience, God's "plan of happiness" is not working for me? What does my worship with God look like when the rain just will not stop? These are questions that I have asked myself. They are questions asked (often silently) by those sitting next to us at church. In some cases, they are the questions that cause some people to abandon religion altogether. In a belief system where finding happiness and joy is seen as the inevitable outcome of faithful living, the lack of happiness and joy can call into question some of our most basic beliefs about ourselves, about our faith community, and about God.

CHAPTER 2

SADNESS ACKNOWLEDGED

SADNESS IN THE SCRIPTURES

The standard works make clear that sadness and suffering are an expected part of life. In fact, gospel teachings suggest that, rather than being an unfortunate accident, the reality of suffering is "baked into" and a necessary part of the plan of salvation. The book of Abraham's account of the premortal existence makes clear that God intended that the spirits who partake in this life would be "proven," a word whose etymological roots suggest both being tried by hard experience and being put to a test, neither of which are particularly joyful and both of which suggest the existence of challenges and trials. That the human experience would be hard, disorienting, and demanding was the very first lesson taught to Adam and Eve after they ate fruit from the tree of knowledge of good and evil. In God's instructions to Adam and Eve, God says that each of them—and by extension, each of us—would be accompanied in life by pain, hard labor, and death (see Genesis 3:16–19). Lehi further elaborates on the impact of Adam and Eve's choice, noting that they and their descendants were destined to know both joy and misery (see 2 Nephi 2:23). But this was not something that Adam and Eve tried to avoid; it was a reality that Adam and Eve both acknowledged and embraced (see Moses 5:11). Life would necessarily be hard and sometimes sorrowful, and that was part of the plan.

SADNESS ACKNOWLEDGED

Even the Book of Mormon's most explicit teaching about the possibility of joy in this life, 2 Nephi 2:25, is clear that joy is not *all* we should expect to experience. In this verse we hear Lehi teaching that "Men [and women] are, that they might have joy" (2 Nephi 2:25). In my experience, Church members often interpret this scriptural phrase to express a sentiment along the lines of:

- Adam and Eve, in their state of innocence, were not capable of experiencing true joy;
- Once Adam and Eve were cast out of the garden, they experienced a wider range of consequences and resulting joy (tied to good choices) and sorrow (tied to bad choices); and
- Like Adam and Eve, when we choose to follow the commandments, we also can experience joy in our lives.

There is nothing incorrect about this reading; it is not inconsistent with the rest of Lehi's teachings from 2 Nephi chapter 2. However, I do think that this summation of what Lehi is teaching misses important nuances that a closer reading of the verse reveals. Specifically, it is my impression that our understanding of Lehi's teaching can be further deepened by looking more closely at Lehi's use of the word "might."

Historically, *might* was the past tense form of the verb *may*, but in 2 Nephi, *might* is used as an auxiliary verb (or helper verb) supporting the verb "have." The word *might*, used in the way Lehi uses it ("men [and women] are, that they *might* have joy") indicates the real possibility of something occurring, or potential that a thing is able to happen. But the word *might* also introduces intentional ambiguity. We deploy the phrase *might have* to express that a thing is able to occur while simultaneously acknowledging that some ambiguity exists. *Might* suggests a reasonable hesitation to avoid jumping to a conclusion too quickly. The word *might* (and the phrase *might have*) is useful for exactly that reason. Its use introduces flexibility—it allows us to make an assertive statement about a past or future event, while also allowing us to openly and honestly acknowledge that uncertainty surrounding the situation continues to exist. Use of the word *might* is an open acknowledgement, and a not very subtle one at that, that something has been made possible, but that the fulfillment of the action is not a foregone conclusion. The word *might*, with all the ambiguity it carries, is part-and-parcel of human existence. We live in a world of *mights*. Lehi's ideas could have been expressed using a variety of other English words or phrases (*shall* have, *will* have, *must* have, *are going to* have, *should* have, etc.), but the best word in this instance was the word *might*. Lehi clearly says joy is now a possibility, but by using the word *might* he also seems to be acknowledging that there will also be times when joy is not present. We do ourselves and others a disservice if we completely ignore the connotations that the word *might* introduces.

Having said all that, I also want to avoid overreading the word *might* to somehow suggest that Lehi is saying that life will be a never-ending series of trials and disappointments with maybe-we-hope-if-we're-lucky a little bit of joy sprinkled in. To the contrary, Lehi's sermon makes clear that joy is something we can expect (note that just before this he says that "Adam fell that [humankind] might be," and we know that this potentiality was indeed realized). In fact, a main thesis in Lehi's sermon is precisely that the outcome of moving from innocence into knowledge was the arrival of pain and also the possibility for joy. Lehi never mentions one without the other. Both pain and joy will come to us during this life.

For Lehi, this was not theoretical theologizing. What we know about Lehi's life indicates that Lehi experienced the broad array of sweet and bitter firsthand. He knew both the feeling of comfort that accompanies revelation and also the pain of rejection by those he loved (see 1 Nephi 1). He both tasted the fruit of the tree of life and experienced overwhelming anxiety for his oldest children and their posterity (see 1 Nephi 8). At the end of his life, he explained that he felt "encircled about eternally in the arms of [God's] love" and also that he was filled with "anxiety" and had a heart "weighed down with sorrow" (2 Nephi 1:15–17). Lehi knew what it felt like to find the promised land but also knew the loss of leaving behind his home and everything that was familiar. Lehi lived a life filled with both joy and misery, and he understood that experiencing sadness and heartache was not an indication of faithlessness or a signal of divine disapproval. Lehi knew, and his life's experience taught him, that sadness, heartache, and misery were just as much a part of human life as happiness, exultation, and joy.

Even more remarkable, Lehi's sermon makes clear that God's plan for humanity *requires* "opposition in all things" (2 Nephi 2:11). Lehi says that not only should we expect both joy and pain, but that God's plan requires that we experience both. This can be a hard thing to hear. Sometimes it feels like a principal goal of life, including in our religious life, is to do those things that will help us avoid sadness. As if somehow a life in which a person seems to escape sorrow is more successful or more fortunate than another person's life in which sorrow is more present. Sometimes, church lessons and sermons seem to suggest (and I like to believe this is unintentional) that if we simply obey the commandments and follow the prophet, we can skirt all the sadness that others who are less faithful or less knowledgeable of God's plan will experience—that the gospel, lived with exact obedience, inoculates us from most (all?) of life's misery. Too often our religious language, either explicitly or implicitly, portrays life as little more than an algorithm. With the right inputs (go to church, pay tithing, etc.) we get the predictably good outputs (happiness, joy, etc.). Kate Bowler framed this approach well when she described a worldview in which "there are spiritual laws that steer the courses of lives and ensure that good things really do happen to good people . . . [and that] in this world there is no such thing as undeserved pain."[1] However, Bowler also goes suggests that, in this view of life, "There is [also] no word for tragedy."[2]

Like Bowler, Elder D. Todd Christofferson rejects this approach since it results in seeing God's plan as little more than "a cosmic vending machine."[3] Lehi's sermon also expressly rejects this premise and, in so doing, guards against seeing sadness and sorrow as an indication of failure (on our part or God's). Lehi argues exactly the opposite, in fact. Consistent with the book of Abraham's observation that life is a place to be "proven," Lehi teaches that in order for agency to be meaningful, we must be able to experience all that this existence has to offer. That means that we should expect to experience a broad array of events in life that bring feelings of joy (like eating mangoes, going to weddings, feeling the sense of God's presence, and so on) and also a similarly broad array of the events in life that bring feelings of misery (like drinking spoiled milk, having a friend die, feeling like God is absent, and so on). Lehi teaches that our eternal growth and development require that we taste both the sweet and the bitter (see 2 Nephi 2:11–15, 23–27). But he makes it clear that we are not left adrift. The Atonement of Jesus Christ can help us get through those hard times and overcome the challenges we face, whether self-inflicted, as a result of others' actions, or just as part of what sometimes happens in life (see 2 Nephi 2:26). But he goes to great pains to teach that we will face times of turmoil and disappointment. Perhaps in more colloquial language, Lehi's sermon might be summarized like this:

- Adam and Eve entered a mortal experience that was rife with challenges. But not only is this okay, this is as it should be. We need these experiences.
- In fact, it is only by knowing bitter that we can know sweet (and vice versa). So, yes, Adam and Eve (and all of us) can now experience misery, but now Adam and Eve (and all of us) can also experience joy. The two are inextricably connected.

- So do not give up hope when sadness and grief arrive—that is to be expected. Because of the Messiah, we have a companion in our sorrows, and we can choose life—even in the darkest hour.

According to Lehi, the good news of Jesus's coming is not that we can now avoid all the vicissitudes of life and sit in a state of permanent joy. Rather, and perhaps paradoxically, the good news is that sadness and happiness are both part of the plan, and that Jesus is ready to walk with us through the full range of experiences on the way to eternal life. In making these observations about the reality that we would face sadness and grief in this life, Lehi was not saying something new (though the clarity of his framing is laudable). In fact, Lehi was reemphasizing something that had been taught and shown time and time again across sacred texts from many different times and places: sometimes, life will be hard. For instance:

- We have already seen that the first lesson Adam and Even learned after eating the fruit of the tree of knowledge of good and evil was the reality of life being filled with hard labor and suffering (see Genesis 3).
- As will be discussed, the Old Testament's collection of psalms contains numerous examples of the psalmist (faithfully) expressing sadness, anger, frustration, and/or mourning at the pain and anguish being experienced in life (depending on how one counts, as many as half of the psalms may fall into this category)—a very short list would include at least Psalms 3, 5, 6, 9, 10, 12, 13, 22, 27, 31, 35, 38, 39, 42, 43, 44, 51, 54, 55, 56, 59, 60, 64, 69, 74, 79, 80, 85, 86, 88, 90, 102, 108, 109, 130, 137, 140, and 143.
- The entirety of Lamentations, usually attributed to the prophet Jeremiah's reaction after viewing the destruction of Jerusalem, is an extended expression of mourning and loss that in the Hebrew is titled simply *'Ekhah,* which translates to "How, or Alas."[4]
- In the Gospel of Matthew's record of the Sermon on the Mount

(Matthew 5–7) and the Gospel of Luke's record of the Sermon on the Plain (Luke 6), Jesus acknowledges the reality that mourning and weeping are part of one's journey of faith (see Matthew 5:4; Luke 6:21).

- Mary and Martha—who were as close to Jesus as anyone—wept at the death of their brother Lazarus and, in a show of boldness only true grief can elicit, both say to Jesus, in effect, "Where were you? If you had been here Lazarus wouldn't have died . . . But you weren't here and now he's dead" (see John 11).
- In multiple parts of the New Testament, believers are taught that tribulation, burden, fear, distress, and sadness are part of discipleship and should be expected (see, for instance, Acts 14:22; Romans 8:18, 35; 12:15; 2 Corinthians 1:3–4; 1 Thessalonians 3:3; Revelation 2:14).
- The Doctrine and Covenants is filled with examples of faithful Saints facing exceptionally challenging circumstances that are the cause of much sorrow and sadness. Most poignantly, section 121 contains what I like to call "Joseph's Lament," in which the first prophet of the Restoration—the one who records multiple face-to-face, personal interactions with Deity and other celestial beings—voices deep and powerful expressions of grief, concern, and mourning (see D&C 121:1–6). The response from God that Joseph receives includes an extended discussion of all the types of tribulations Joseph might expect to suffer (see D&C 122:5–9).
- In the Pearl of Great Price, we have a record of Enoch's vision of humanity, which included a vision of the Flood. At seeing the Flood and the loss of life it entailed, Enoch "had bitterness of soul, and wept over his brethren, and said unto the heavens: I will refuse to be comforted" (Moses 7:44). A few verses later, it is recorded that Enoch hears the *earth itself* mourning, with these words: "Wo, wo is me, the mother of men; I am pained, I am weary" (v. 48).

SADNESS ACKNOWLEDGED

- The Book of Mormon contains multiple accounts of the faithful feeling grief, pain, sadness, and sorrow. I have already referenced Lehi's feeling of sadness over his sons Laman and Lemuel, which is expressed numerous times throughout 1 and 2 Nephi. In addition to that, consider:

    - The "psalm of Nephi," in which he grieves the death of his father and expresses sorrow for his shortcomings (see 2 Nephi 4).
    - Jacob's constant anxiety and fear for his people (see 2 Nephi 6:3; Jacob 1:5; 2:3; 4:8) and his concluding reflections that the Nephites were "a lonesome and a solemn people, wanderers, cast out from Jerusalem, born in tribulation, in a wilderness, and hated of our brethren . . . ; wherefore, we did mourn out our days" (Jacob 7:26).
    - The obvious distress and sadness that permeates Moroni's writing at the end of his life, including this observation following the last battle in which he participated: "Behold, the Nephites who had escaped into the country southward were hunted by the Lamanites, until they were all destroyed. And my father also was killed by them, and I even remain alone to write the sad tale of the destruction of my people. But behold, they are gone, and I fulfil the commandment of my father. And whether they will slay me, I know not. Therefore I will write and hide up the records in the earth; and whither I go it mattereth not" (Mormon 8:2–4).

This is a wildly incomplete list. In fact, it is only the tip of the iceberg. But this admittedly incomplete list is sufficient to make the point: *Sacred text is not shy about acknowledging that sadness and sorrow are part of life—no one is exempt.* And once one starts to recognize its presence in scriptures . . . It. Is. Everywhere. This is not to say there is no joy and happiness in the scriptures—there is plenty of that too—but those who compiled our sacred texts chose to include, among the teachings and experiences that constitute our scripture, the hard stuff of life. Sadness, sorrow, grief, and pain are as much a part of our sacred tradition and history as happiness and joy are. The Old Testament's book of Ecclesiastes articulates this reality most succinctly. In chapter 3, verses 1 and 4, Koheleth states, "To every thing there is a season, and a time to every purpose under the heaven: . . . A time to weep, and a time to laugh; a time to mourn, and a time to dance."[5] Just like life will have laughing and dancing, we should expect that life will have weeping and wailing. Far from being a signal of unrighteousness or faithlessness, there is a "season" and "a time" for both. Laughing and dancing, weeping and wailing. They are not optional—they *will* happen. We will know sorrow. It is simply part of the human condition. And the fact that sadness, sorrow, grief, and pain are in our sacred text should signal to us that there is something about those feelings which makes them just as sacred as their more pleasant counterparts.

DIVINE PASSIBILITY

One of the beautiful truths of the restored gospel is that we know God and Jesus feel emotions, including sadness, sorrow, grief, and pain. This truth runs contrary to those ideas about God that are articulated in documents like the Westminster Confession, which states that God is "a most pure spirit, invisible, without body, parts, or passions." The intent of such statements was likely to insulate God from being impacted by human action/inaction or "mere emotions." This notion, "impassibility" (that is the theological term for this idea), kept God separate from humankind and thus preserved the "otherness" and sovereignty of God. For Latter-day Saints, however, far from being something that makes our God and Jesus less "godly," it is, in fact, their deep emotional connection with us that serves as a foundation for our faith in them. While there are many examples of this, a few specific and poignant examples are sufficient here.

In Enoch's vision, mentioned earlier, as he is seeing the conditions of humankind that precipitated the Flood, Enoch observes something that stops him dead in his tracks. The record states: "The God of heaven looked upon the residue of the people, and he wept" (Moses 7:28). Enoch does not know how to process this. He asks, "How is it that the heavens weep, and shed forth their tears as the rain upon the mountains? . . . How is it that thou canst weep, seeing thou art holy, and from all eternity to all eternity? . . . How is it thou canst weep?" (Moses 7:28, 29, 31). It seems that perhaps Enoch conceptualized a God who is unaffected by what happens on earth; a God who is unruffled no matter what transpires, or—maybe even more problematically—who is always "happy" regardless of the situation. Maybe some of us still do. (It is worth noting that if one sees God as never sad, then it is easy to see why weeping, or any emotions that might elicit weeping, would be considered a weakness. If we are to emulate a stoic God, then emotion—particularly, sadness—is to be avoided and is potentially viewed as sinful and/or faithless.) But this is not the God that Enoch encounters, and this is not the God of the Latter-day Saints. Enoch meets a God who weeps. This is a life-changing revelation for Enoch.[6] And it remains an important invitation for all of us to embrace the same kind of emotional vulnerability that God models.

In answer to Enoch's question ("How is it thou canst weep?"), Enoch receives the response from God that "these thy brethren . . . are the workmanship of mine own hands" who, as a result of their own agency, "are without affection, and they hate their own blood" and have fallen under condemnation and are now suffering. Thus, says God, "The whole heavens shall weep over them . . . ; wherefore should not the heavens weep, seeing these shall suffer?" (Moses 7:32, 33, 37). In short, God loves them and it hurts God to see this creation suffer—even when the source of their suffering in this circumstance was their own poor choices. If the God who is holy and from all eternity to all eternity can feel the emotions that lead to weeping as "rain upon the mountains" (v. 28), then those emotions must also, by definition, be holy. For me, this is still a staggering revelation.

However, Enoch's vision is not the only example of divine passibility. We also see this in the Gospels, which describe Jesus's life in the Holy Land. These records show that Jesus, whose life was perfect, who not only stayed on the covenant path but who actually formed the covenant path, felt sadness, sorrow, grief, and pain. As already noted earlier, Jesus's teachings included a recognition that mourning and weeping would be part of our life's journey. Jesus was no exception to this truth. In fact, leaning on the language of Isaiah, we often describe Jesus as "a man of sorrows, and acquainted with grief" (Isaiah 53:3). Consider the feelings that lay beneath Jesus's reaction to the death of Lazarus. It is recorded that when approaching Lazarus's tomb, Jesus "groaned within himself." Other English translations of this verse render the underlying Greek "again greatly disturbed" (New Revised Standard Version, NRSV) or "being deeply moved" (New American Standard Bible) or "once more deeply moved" (New International Version). In other words, he felt sadness and grief. Upon seeing the suffering of Mary and Martha at the death of their brother, and after arriving at the place where his friend Lazarus had been laid to rest, perhaps the most well-known New Testament scripture records, "Jesus wept" (John 11:35). It is striking that Jesus's weeping and feelings of sadness occurred despite the fact that just prior to this moment, Jesus had taught Mary and Marth about the reality of the resurrection (see John 11:25–26) and that just following this moment Jesus would bring Lazarus out of the grave (see John 11:44). So, even while knowing that Lazarus would shortly be brought back to life and eventually resurrected, Jesus was *still* moved to tears at the loss of a friend and the suffering felt by those who also loved Lazarus.

Similarly, we see the Jesus who was acquainted with sorrow and grief as Jesus's earthly ministry was coming to a close. The Gospels of both Matthew and Luke record what is often called "Jesus's lament over Jerusalem." This moment is captured in Greg Olsen's painting *O Jerusalem*, which hangs in many Latter-day Saint homes. Though the language in Matthew and Luke is slightly different, the message is the same; Jesus is expressing sorrow and grief—he is lamenting—that the children of Jerusalem would not heed his message and be gathered. Luke records Jesus's language this way: "How often have I desired to gather your children together as a hen gathers her brood under her wings, and you were not willing" (Luke 13:34, NRSV). It is touching not only that Jesus feels such sorrow but also that Jesus voices these feelings in such an intimate, personal way. It is a lament that reveals an exceptional depth of emotion. With words like "how often" and "desire," we understand that this is not a one-time feeling, but something that Jesus felt throughout his ministry; a feeling that has motivated him. And by invoking the image of a hen gathering her brood, Jesus reveals the type of care, and even longing, he felt toward those whom he was serving. He, like a hen, just wanted to protect those to whom he ministered. Consider the tenderness this image invokes and the sentiment, the deeply felt emotions, that this image brings to our hearts. And with the final phrase, "You were not willing," we are privy to the sense of sadness and grief that Jesus must have felt in that moment. "I tried," Jesus seemed to say, "and you just wouldn't listen." It is not recorded that Jesus also wept in this moment, but it is not that much of a stretch to imagine that he did.

Jesus's passibility is also evident in the Book of Mormon's recounting of his visit to the people at the temple in Bountiful following three days of darkness and upheaval. After Jesus finished his initial instruction to the people—which included instruction about the reality of mourning as part of earthly existence (see 3 Nephi 12:4)—it is recorded that Jesus healed the sick and afflicted and then invited the little children to be brought forward (see 3 Nephi 17:7–11). With the little children at his feet, and surrounded by a kneeling throng, "Jesus groaned within himself, and said: Father, I am troubled because of the wickedness of the people of the house of Israel" (3 Nephi 17:14). I find it truly remarkable, after all Jesus had done—recall this scene occurs *after* he had been resurrected—that (1) Jesus still feels the kind sorrow and grief that results in a groan of sadness, and (2) Jesus openly expresses that sorrow and grief to God, and in front of a multitude. Not only is Jesus unafraid of feeling troubled, but he is also fearless in his expression of it. We do not know what Jesus says next, but we know that he prays with such feeling and conviction that "no tongue can speak, neither can there be written by any man, neither can the hearts of men conceive so great and marvelous things as we both saw and heard Jesus speak" (3 Nephi 17:17). My sense is, given the reaction of the people, that the "great and marvelous things" Jesus spoke were probably filled with emotional energy—they were the expressions of one who feels things deeply.

From my perspective, perhaps the most remarkable moment in which we witness Jesus's passibility comes on the cross. I want to be careful in what I am trying to say here. We know that in the process of Atonement, Jesus suffered "pains and afflictions and temptations of every kind . . . that the word might be fulfilled which saith he will take upon him the pains and the sicknesses of his people" (Alma 7:11). Borrowing from the words of Isaiah, we understand that through the Atonement, Jesus "hath borne our griefs, and carried our sorrows" (Isaiah 53:4). Both of these scriptures make clear that Jesus's Atonement included feeling and carrying *others'* sorrow and grief. Jesus is, thereby, with us, in *our* pain, affliction, temptations, grief, and sorrows, "which suffering caused myself [Jesus], even God, the greatest of all, to tremble because of pain, and to bleed at every pore, and to suffer both body and spirit" (D&C 19:18). As the famous song goes, when I think of Jesus, "our burden gladly bearing," it makes my heart simultaneously sing and break. I cannot always tell what kind of tears, joyous or crestfallen, accompany my use of the phrase, "My God, how great thou art."

SADNESS ACKNOWLEDGED

Though all of this is true, it is not what I want to highlight. What is sometimes overlooked in the discussion of Christ's Passion is that in addition to bearing *our* griefs and burdens, Jesus also—consistent with the mortality he experienced—grappled with his *own* griefs and burdens. I believe this is most evident on the cross.

In the Gospels of Mark and Matthew, there are parallel descriptions of the moment of Jesus's death. In that moment, according to these two sources, Jesus cried out loudly, "Eli, Eli, lama sabachthani?" or, "My God, my God, why hast thou forsaken me?" (Matthew 27:46; see also Mark 15:34; Mark uses "Eloi" instead of "Eli"). Likely spoken in Aramaic—which would have been the language most common among those with whom Jesus associated—this was a direct reference to Psalm 22. Jesus was never one to reference scripture unintentionally, so looking at the rest of this psalm gives us insight into how Jesus himself may have been feeling. In this psalm, which has moments that are heartbreaking, we see clear expressions of sadness and grief. Looking back at Jesus on the cross, it is easy to see how this language might have resonated with Jesus's personal feelings at that moment:

> *My God, my God, why hast thou forsaken me?*
> *   why art thou so far from helping me, and from the words of*
> *   my roaring?*
> *O my God, I cry in the daytime, but thou hearest not;*
> *   and in the night season, and am not silent. . . .*
> *All they that see me laugh me to scorn . . .*
> *Be not far from me; for trouble is near;*
> *   for there is none to help. . . .*
> *I am poured out like water, and all my bones are out of joint:*
> *   my heart is like wax; it is melted in the midst of my bowels.*
> *My strength is dried up like a potsherd [a broken piece of*
> *   pottery];*

> *and my tongue cleaveth to my jaws; and thou hast brought me into the dust of death. . . .*
>
> *They part my garments among them, and cast lots upon my vesture.*
>
> *But be not thou far from me, O Lord: O my strength, haste thee to help me.*
>
> (Psalm 22:1–2, 7, 11, 14–15, 18–19)

As I just noted, I think it is fair to assume that perhaps Jesus's invoking of this particular psalm while on the cross was intentional. And I think that this intentionality points to more than just the burden Jesus bore for us. I think it gives a clue as to how Jesus—the man—felt in that moment. Touchingly, this psalm is the only place in the entire Old Testament where the use of the Hebrew *'eli* is doubled.[7] "My God, my God . . ." he cried out. Like the psalmist before him, in this moment, Jesus seemed to feel a sense of being alone and abandoned. And through this brief but powerful reference to Psalm 22, Jesus aroused images and language that describe a real and visceral sense of grief and sorrow.

To be clear, this is not to say that some of the abandonment Jesus might have felt was not also part of his atoning work. Of this moment, Elder Jeffrey R. Holland explained: "That the supreme sacrifice of His Son might be as complete as it was voluntary and solitary, the Father briefly withdrew from Jesus the comfort of His Spirit, the support of His personal presence. It was required, indeed it was central to the significance of the Atonement, that this perfect Son who had never spoken ill nor done wrong nor touched an unclean thing had to know how the rest of humankind—us, all of us—would feel when we did commit such sins. For His Atonement to be infinite and eternal, He had to feel what it was like to die not only physically but spiritually, to sense what it was like to have the divine Spirit withdraw, leaving one feeling totally, abjectly, hopelessly alone."[8] For Jesus to be able to "know according to the flesh how to succor his people according to their infirmities" (Alma 7:12), he had to know what it was like to be cut off from God. As Barbara Brown Taylor said it, "In the silence [from God] surrounding his death, Jesus became the best possible companion for those whose prayers are not answered, who would give anything just to hear God call them by name. Him too. He wanted that too, and he did not get it. What he got, instead, was a fathomless silence in which to cry out."[9] But, while it may be true that Jesus's sense of abandonment helps him help us, that does not preclude nor foreclose the reality that this distance from God was also *personally* challenging for Jesus and resulted in Jesus *personally* feeling sorrow and grief. The language of the psalm, expressed entirely in the first person (I/me), must have had a powerful meaning to Jesus or he would not have used his few remaining breaths to reference it. I believe Jesus's intentional use of this psalm points, at least in part, to the feelings of sadness, grief, sorrow, abandonment, and isolation he personally felt as he hung on a Roman tool of torture.

SADNESS AND GRIEF: PART OF GOD'S PLAN

As noted earlier, loss, disaster, and tragedy in infinite variations of scale, intensity, and duration occur in life. And when those things occur, they invite feelings of sorrow, grief, pain, despair, and misery. Far from being an indication of faithlessness or sin, they are not only part of life but a vital component of the plan of salvation. We *need* sadness, grief, and sorrow. This is a simple and hard truth. Our own lives evince the ubiquity of these emotions. Our sacred texts acknowledge and sacralize these feelings through the stories and teachings of those whom we find in their pages. Even descriptions of God and Jesus include examples where they experience sorrow and grief. And yet, even with this overwhelming testimony to the sacred nature of these emotions, we live in a culture that sometimes suggests that we should avoid suffering. As Elder Jeffrey R. Holland explains, we live in a "modern world when many have come to believe that the highest good in life is to avoid all suffering."[10] Whether the ideal is to avoid all suffering or to maintain a stiff upper lip in the face of suffering—ours or someone else's—it seems some believe that it is an indication of spiritual righteousness and strength to remain unfazed. Yet, this is not so. As one commentator put it, "To hide from suffering and death would be an act of denial."[11]

This recognition requires within us a dramatic recalibration of perspective with regard to what faith and worship look like within a community of believers. Faith and worship during the good times is easy to imagine. Praise comes naturally when things are going smoothly. But what do faith and worship look like when things are not going smoothly? What does it mean to have faith and worship when the world we know is crumbling around us? In the face of crippling loss, disaster, and tragedy, when feelings of sorrow, grief, pain, despair, and misery are more than annoying flies buzzing around our otherwise-unaffected reserve of faith, and are, instead, so overwhelming that they block out the sun entirely, such that we no longer know what it is like to live with the sun in our view—then what? What does it mean to have faith and worship when we no longer even have the language to express our pain? What do faith and worship look like when loss, disaster, and tragedy have shaken the very core of our belief?

Some may think, and we may even have been taught, that we have to get beyond our feelings of sorrow, grief, pain, despair, and misery in order to return to faith and worship. That somehow, we must first resolve challenges and return to a happy and joyful state before we can really worship properly. But that simply is not true. Rather, our sacred texts recognize that we can faithfully express sadness as part of worship—we can lament. As Michael Card puts it, "Lament is not a path *to* worship, but the path *of* worship."[12] And, as has already been noted and will be discussed in more detail, sacred texts are full of laments of various kinds. Thus, much of what is covered in this chapter (and this book) can be reduced to this simple observation: If the hard and difficult parts of life and the feelings those events elicit are just as holy and just as important as happy and joyful moments—and our sacred texts make clear that they are—then if our worship is to be authentic, we must also make room to include expressions of sadness and grief from a foundation of faith. Let me say that again with a different formulation: If pain and misery are part of the human and divine experience, then our faith must be big enough to include language that expresses sorrow, grief, pain, and despair as part of worship. Said one more time, even more directly: *Expressing sadness and grief can be an act of faith and worship.*

A BRIEF DIVERSION ON THE GENRE OF LAMENT

FIRST THINGS FIRST . . .

Having introduced the term *lament*, it seems useful to pause for a moment to address a few important items to level-set the conversation and establish a foundation for the discussion of lament that is to follow.

Item one: Throughout the remaining chapters, there will be several references to "Israel" and the "sacred tradition" that the Latter-day Saints (and other Christians) have inherited. I am optimistic that such references have two impacts. First, as a matter of trajectory, one purpose of this book is to show that the things discussed herein are as ancient as is our knowledge of God. These are not newfangled, new-age ideas that have only come in vogue as of late. Rather, these things are, and have always been, pivotal when it comes to maintaining a relationship with God and with each other: lament is part of covenant keeping.

And that leads to a related point. In my view, the term *Israel* is deeply connected with the term *covenant*. After all, a defining characteristic of Israel is its ongoing covenant relationship with God. Though some of the texts referenced in this book are exceptionally old chronologically (e.g., the stories in Exodus go back thousands of years), the covenants that undergird these texts are as fresh today as they have ever been. Thus, "Israel" is often used herein to mean, in essence, anyone in

A BRIEF DIVERSION ON THE GENRE OF LAMENT

a covenant relationship with the God of Abraham, Isaac, and Jacob. In saying this, I am not intending to crowd out modern-day Jews or other Christians; only to say that Latter-day Saint theology also includes a self-understanding of having, as a defining characteristic, a covenant relationship with God. Thus, when I speak of Israel I am thinking of the people that Moses led out of Egypt (and their descendants) just as much as I am thinking of those folks who bind themselves to God via baptism today.

Item two: I want to be clear that murmuring and lament are two different things.[1] In my mind, Elder Neal A. Maxwell's October 1989 general conference address, "Murmur Not,"[2] gave murmuring its most thorough treatment. In that talk, he explains that murmuring is "half-suppressed resentment or muttered complaint" and that the murmurer "often lacks the courage to express openly his [or her] concerns" and "regards any response . . . as hostile."[3] This is exactly the opposite of lament. Where murmuring is half-suppressed resentment *about* God (often intended to provoke others), lament is fully open expression *to* God from the midst of sadness and grief. Contrary to murmuring, which does not seek a response, lament is foundationally premised on the trust that God will respond and on a conviction of God's loving-kindness, concern, and ability to act in our behalf. I will not spend more time on this, but I wanted to briefly highlight that murmuring and lament could not be more dissimilar.

Item three: In this book I will talk about "laments" as a genre: i.e., what they are, their basic structure, and how they are used. This is intended to be only a basic introduction to lament—the body of literature on lament language generally and the lament psalms specifically is vast (and growing). For the purpose of this brief introduction, I will largely focus on the lament psalms, though, as has been acknowledged, we see laments in many places other than the collection of psalms in the Old Testament (and, on the flip side, there are many psalms that are not laments). By focusing on the Psalter initially, and more narrowly on lament psalms, we can build a framework for what lament is and how it can be faithfully employed, which will then inform the broader discussion about lament that will follow.

Finally, item four: Some of the things we will consider together may feel emotionally heavy. Perhaps that has already been the case. After all, in order to explore lament, we also need to discuss loss, disaster, and tragedy. That may stir up emotions that arise from our own encounters with loss, disaster, and tragedy. I know this from experience. More than once—all alone in my small office (often in the late night/early morning hours)—I broke down and typed through tears as I worked through the raw emotions that these topics elicit. But I believe deeply in the power of lament, so I know that sorrow, grief, and pain are both part of all of our lives' journeys and critical to our ongoing progression and growth. So, allow the feelings to come. When we claim these hard feelings and take them to God (i.e., when we lament), they can foster a more authentic and deepened covenant relationship with God. In chapter 6—after we have done the work of exploring the topic of lament using ancient scriptures and modern-day insights and teachings—I will offer some specific ideas on how to implement this principle "in real life." When we get there, and with the firm grounding in lament the intervening chapters will establish, I hope those concrete suggestions will be helpful guides to channeling some of these emotions and, more generally, to claiming the power of lament in each of our lives. What's more, in chapter 7 I will reflect on the reality that lament does not persist forever and discuss the deliverance and newness that accompanies lament. All that to say, hang in there, even if it gets difficult; it is worth it.

Now, let us press forward.

THE PSALTER

The book of Psalms, often called the Psalter, is a collection of religious poetry (or songs) that contains a variety of different types

A BRIEF DIVERSION ON THE GENRE OF LAMENT

of psalms, including lament psalms. In the *Come, Follow Me—For Individuals and Families: Old Testament 2022* materials, it says that the psalms give us "a window into the soul of God's ancient people . . . how they felt about God, what they worried about, and how they found peace."[4] Of the psalms generally, Brueggemann observes, "The Psalms crave for and mediate communion with God, but Israel insists that this communion be honest, open to criticism, and capable of transformation."[5] It is in part because the Psalter is a collection of *poetic* expressions that it has the ability to do just this—the Psalter breaks through the sometimes-staid language of clergy and fosters honest communion that is capable of transformation. It is also why the psalms, which have special relevance even today, have always had a place in worship going back millennia. Most scholars believe that psalms and religious poetry (which may have been voiced as songs) served a formal, liturgical purpose for Israel that pre-dates the Davidic Kingdom (indeed, one of the oldest portions of text in the Old Testament, the Song of the Sea, Exodus 15:1–18, is reasonably considered a psalm). That is to say, just as the Church of Jesus Christ uses specific songs as opening hymns, sacrament hymns, or Christmas hymns, or just as it uses formal (often set) language in various parts of our worship practices, psalms were used by Israel, both communally and individually, in religious settings as part of their worship practices.

Like Latter-day Saints' hymns and set prayers, the psalms provided Israel formal mechanisms to engage in God-talk. As Latter-day Saint scholar John Hilton III noted pithily, the psalms "provide powerful language of worship."[6] But not just any language: open, honest, transformative God-talk. In modern times, the Psalter continues to serve this purpose. Members of ancient and modern monasteries recite the psalms on a set schedule.[7] Modern-day Jews and Christians include the psalms in their sacred traditions and celebrations. All this to say, the Psalter has provided worship language for thousands of years precisely because, as a collection of poetry, it has a proclivity for unvarnished expression. Though terminology varies slightly among different scholars, the Psalter contains psalms of praise, wisdom, thanksgiving, and enthronement in addition to psalms of lament, each serving a purpose and each offering a different "mode" of worship that is open, honest, and potentially transformative.[8]

THE GENRE OF LAMENT

As odd as it may sound initially, laments are a genre of worship. What is a genre? Genres are expressions that follow a predictable form and structure, even if the specifics of individual expressions differ from each other. Consider, for instance, the genre of movies colloquially called "romantic comedies." Movies in this genre all follow the same basic form and structure: two people meet, they develop feelings for each other, they face a challenge, they overcome that challenge. The details of each story may vary, but we all know the general framework. Whether it is *Roman Holiday*, *You've Got Mail*, or *While You Were Sleeping*, we know what to expect. And that is partially what makes them fun to watch. The same is generally true of all genres—fantasy, sci-fi, action/adventure, sitcom, procedural drama, young adult fiction, and so on. Each genre has its own "rules" that provide form and structure to the story. The details vary, but within each genre, stories generally follow a predictable story arc. This is not bad. The rules of a given genre *do not* inhibit the authenticity of the story. Rather, the generic conventions serve as a tool to help the story unfold. Genres are the frameworks upon which expressions are built.

Applied to the language of worship, one genre is lament. Just as praise is one *type* of worship, lament is also a type of worship. Laments are a type of language used to express faith and that have a largely predictable form and structure, even if the specific details of different laments differ from each other. Laments are the genre of worship employed to complain to God. The fact that laments have a form and structure does not inhibit the authenticity of the complaint; rather, it serves to support the articulation of the complaint as a form of worship. Specific to this discussion, it is critical to recognize that because the Latter-day Saints' standard works include the Psalter (and numerous other examples of laments), within the Latter-day Saint faith tradition we have a genre of worship language for faithful, honest, open complaint to God. In moments of crushing pain and grief, we can worship through lament. Soong-Chan Rah explains, "[Lament] is the human response to anguish and adversity, and is not bound by the rules of praise. . . . The lamenter is allowed to express indignation and even outrage about the experience of suffering. The lamenter talks back to God and ultimately petitions him for help, in the midst of pain."[9] Foundational to the use of lament in worship is the belief that by articulating our pain to God, faithfully, honestly, and openly, we are able to turn that pain over to God, which then creates conditions that allow us, eventually, to relinquish that pain.[10]

THE STRUCTURE OF LAMENT

If laments are one genre of worship found in the Psalter, then it must be the case that lament psalms should follow a generally shared form and structure. And they do. To be clear, not every lament psalm looks exactly the same, but they do have recognizable elements in common. I find Denise Dombkowski Hopkins's outlining of the lament psalms to be the most instructive and easy to follow. This comes from her book *Journey Through the Psalms* and is a snapshot of how the laments are generally structured.[11]

1. Address
    a. Short, emotion-packed
    b. Why? How long?
2. Complaint proper
    a. The psalmists suffering (I/we)
    b. The enemies (they)

      c. God accused of not caring/doing (you)
3. Petition
4. Motivations
      a. Confession of sin
      b. Protestation of innocence
      c. Public relations value of psalmist

5. Confession of trust
      a. Usually introduced by *but*
      b. Faith that knows what it is talking about
6. Vow of praise

Of this structure, Dombkowski Hopkins offers this concise and informative commentary: "As can be seen from its structure, a lament does not merely bemoan hardship, but rather seeks change. . . . A lament psalm describes a distress, interprets it, and appeals to God based on that interpretation. The psalmist's intention is to motivate God's intervention. In order to motivate, lament language is vivid and metaphorical, evocative and provocative. It seeks God's involvement to change the situation of distress. Lament language is intense because it is language of the extremities of life, language in the pit of disorientation. If we are to enter the world of lament, we must enter into the intensity and emotion of lament poetry, rather than judge it or be shocked by it."[12] Following this brief introduction to form and structure, Dombkowski Hopkins's book explores each component of a lament psalm that she identifies. Her analysis is more detailed than is needed here, but I recommend her work to anyone seeking additional insight about the psalms generally and laments specifically. Dombkowski Hopkins, a former teacher of mine, is as wise as she is profound, and she has a personal and artistic approach to her analysis that is unique.

A BRIEF DIVERSION ON THE GENRE OF LAMENT

It is sufficient to note a few key observations about the structure of lament that will inform the chapters that follow:

- First, as the structure above makes clear, the Psalter's language of complaint (and, often, lament language outside the Psalter) is stylized. There is a formula for how it is done. The existence of a form provides a framework upon which one can "hang" the details of a specific situation. In a sense, the generic conventions of a lament psalm provide a guide for how one can complain to God in faith. Implicit in this stylization is acknowledgment that (1) worship, including the formal worship that might occur in a sacred space in the presence of others, should encompass lament. There would be no need to develop a stylistic method for expressing lamentation if faithful worship did not demand it. And (2) there is enough of a need for the language of lament that a stylized form for such language proves useful. If only one or only two people in the history of worship needed to express lament, then it is unlikely that a stylized lament genre would have developed. The fact that psalms of lament exist is a signal that the entire worship community needs (or may eventually need) psalms of lament.
- Second, the language of the lament psalms includes language that expressly describes the suffering being experienced and the way in which this suffering impacts the sufferers' sense of relationship with God. This language, as Dombkowski Hopkins says, is often "evocative and provocative." But this rawness is part of the value the lament psalms offer. The voice of grief—as was shown above in the instance of Mary and Martha challenging Jesus's absence while Lazarus died—is often unfiltered and bold. Rather than being embarrassed by such language, or, even worse, dismissing it as weakness, the lament psalms call us to feel what the psalmist felt and then to honor those feelings by letting the language of grief and sorrow stand proudly next to language of praise and exultation. It

is precisely from the boldness of lament—evocative and provocative as it sometimes is—that the lament psalms draw their power. And it is in our honoring of that boldness that we show respect to the psalmist (and all for whom the psalmist's words resonate) and create the opportunity for community.

- Third, just as life varies, the lament psalms vary. Within the genre of lament, scholars have further codified laments into smaller categories (into psalms of communal lament or individual lament, for instance). My point is that the experience of sorrow and grief may be common to all humankind, but the details of that sorrow and grief are unique. Like fingerprints, each moment of sorrow and grief, whether experienced by a community (e.g., the United States upon hearing of the massacre in Newtown, Connecticut) or an individual (e.g., a parent of one of the children killed in Newtown) is unique and, in that sense, hallowed. The fact that laments come in different lengths, using different language, voicing different concerns, and asking for different kinds of assistance from God should signal to us that there is no one way to lament. The variety of lament psalms speaks to the variety of human experience and should empower us to feel what we feel without reservation or comparison.

- Lastly, every lament psalm, except one, has what is sometimes called the "turn"—the moment in the psalm when the psalmist moves from lament and into what Dombkowski Hopkins labels a "confession of trust" (you will see in her outline above, this turn is demarked by the dotted line). For Latter-day Saints, the "turn" that might most readily come to mind is not found in the Psalter, but in 2 Nephi 4—the psalm of Nephi. In verses 16–19, Nephi expresses grief at his weaknesses (he laments). It is a bold, and frankly uncharacteristic, admission on Nephi's part. But later in verse 19, we see the turn: "Nevertheless, I know in whom I have trusted." And for the remaining sixteen verses, Nephi offers a

A BRIEF DIVERSION ON THE GENRE OF LAMENT

"faith that knows what it's talking about" (to use Dombkowski Hopkins's language) and concludes with statements of praise and vows of commitment. The same is true of every lament psalm in the Psalter, except one. The fact of the turn in lament psalms seems to suggest that the process of lament is a process of healing. Only Psalm 88 does not have the turn. That psalm begins and ends with lament. But even this is instructive. The inclusion of Psalm 88 in our sacred text seems to acknowledge that much of the time (maybe even most of the time) lament can turn to thanksgiving. But sometimes—not often, but sometimes—even complaining in faith is not enough to escape the sorrow we feel. Oddly, perhaps, I find deep reservoirs of hope in the reality that even Psalm 88 has a place in the Psalter, because it means there is room for everyone in our sacred tradition. I will more closely examine Psalm 88 in chapter 3.

Though it may seem counterintuitive to those used to hearing only messages of hope and gladness at church, the act of complaining in faith—the act of lament—has a role in our worship that is recognized by our sacred texts and traditions. Lament plays a meaningful role in the process of coming to God and is critically important in a world filled with grief. Michael Card summarized the value of laments well. He says, "The language of lament gives a meaningful form to our grief by providing a vocabulary for our suffering and then offering it to God as worship."[13] Lament is worship just as much as praise is. It is an unfortunate reality, though, that many of us have not learned how to use this particular tool.

CHAPTER 3

WORSHIPPING THROUGH LAMENT

THE NATURE OF WORSHIP

It should be clear by now that I believe worship can and should infuse every component of our lives. Worship is not something we "do" on Sunday. It is a way of being. I connect deeply with Abraham Heschel's way of describing worship. Heschel says worship is living such that "the question about God becomes an inescapable concern. . . . Such ultimate concern is *an act of worship*, an act of acknowledging in the most intense manner the supremacy of the issue."[1] Since his use of the word "question" might be a bit confusing for some, let me pause for a moment. *Question* in the way that Heschel uses it does not mean interrogate, but rather being receptive or being open to. It is "question" in the sense of "ready to hear." Perhaps the best synonym for the word *question* in the way Heschel is using it is the Hebrew word *hineni,* "here I am," which signals an openness and willingness, a readiness of sorts (this is how Moses, Abraham, Samuel, and Isaiah all responded to God's call; they responded with *hineni,* "here I am"). Thus, Heschel suggests that worship is when the willingness to be open to dialogue with God becomes "inescapable."

Bishop Dean M. Davies strikes a similar note by describing worship as including the sense of yearning, a desire to approach God, and being drawn to God.[2] Worship is when uncovering God in our lives, even for a fleeting moment, becomes the ultimate concern. Worship is, foundationally, a longing for God. This is what Heschel means when he talks of "the question about God." With this in mind, it seems there are few things more worshipful than entering into a dialogue with God with the words "why" and "how" on our lips.

Heschel's explanation of worship makes clear to us that the "question about God," this ultimate concern, can come to us at many points in life—good and bad. Consider: there are few times more joyous than when a child is welcomed into a home (through birth, adoption, or foster care), and in this moment when we often are driven "in the most intense manner" to dialogue with God—this is worship. The same is true at weddings, when bonds of love are created, and at funerals, when bonds of love are stretched across eternities. The same is true when we summit a high mountain peak and look out over the vast expanse of an unfolding valley below us. Or as we bob gently on a boat in the middle of a lake with the moon rising over the horizon. Or when we first learn that a loved one has a disease that will cause them to depart this earth. Or when we finally slow down enough to appreciate the staggering beauty of an acorn or to savor the juicy goodness of a ripe orange or to let the song of a bird and the babble of a creek echo in our soul. Or when we reflect on the atrocities committed by one human against another during war. Or when an unexpected act of kindness on the part of another meets an unvoiced need of our own. Or when a cherished idea or relationship crumbles before our eyes.

All this to say that once we understand worship as synonymous with the moments when our "question about God" is the "ultimate concern"—once we see worship as the moments in life that drive our gaze to God—then it is clear that worship can infuse every component of existence. Authentic, true, honest worship is as expansive as our experiences—even sorrow and grief. And in those moments of sorrow and grief, when our gaze is turned heavenward and we boldly ask the "question about God"—in other words, when we worship—that worship can be expressed through the language of lament.

THE UNCOMFORTABLENESS OF LAMENT

If my years of church attendance are in any way reflective of others' experiences, it seems that it is often much easier for individuals at church to express their happiness and gladness than it is to express other emotions. It seems easier to voice our worship in those moments when the "question about God" leads to statements of praise like "I do not understand why I am so blessed!" I do not know whether it is a learned behavior or whether there is an innate sense that some things are too intimate to be voiced, but it is often harder for individuals to express sadness and sorrow, particularly when those hard emotions are directed toward God. It is rare that someone uses language like this in a church service:

> *Be gracious to me, O LORD, for I am languishing;*
> *O LORD, heal me, for my bones are shaking with terror.*
> *My soul also is struck with terror,*
> *while you, O LORD—how long?*
>
> (PSALM 6:2–3, NRSV)

Instead, at those times when our worship might lead us to make statements of lament, the feelings of grief and sorrow are often pushed down and kept behind a well-ironed white shirt or freshly ruffled skirt and away from public view. They are words we are afraid to speak.

And yet, avoiding lament really only hurts ourselves and our community. Without the ability to lament there is, as Brueggemann puts it, a "loss of *genuine covenant interaction*" because the petitioner "has become voiceless or has a voice that is permitted to speak only praise. This," he says, "does not square with reality" because "covenant minus lament is finally a practice of denial, cover-up, and pretense."[3]

Said more starkly, Michael Card asserts, "Our refusal to lament . . . separates us from God."[4] When praise may not be forthcoming, the inability or unwillingness to use lament renders us voiceless in moments of sorrow and grief. The inability or unwillingness to lament threatens to de-link us from God, because without lament our connection with Deity is inauthentic and partial. Rather than a relationship grounded in raw openness, our supposed relationship becomes a performance. Rather than simply acknowledging to God our feelings (which God already knows), we hold something back, pretending to be other than we are. A lack of lament leads to a situation where socially driven ideas of orthopraxy (the "right way to worship") trump true, honest, open covenant relationship.

If we are to have a true covenant relationship with Deity, we must have true lament. Perhaps it is time to see laments for what they are. And what are they? Michael Card answers this question powerfully: "Within each of us lies a hidden Holy of Holies . . . our laments are that most sacred space."[5] Laments, because they reveal the deepest part of our soul, are "that most sacred space," truly our personal "Holy of Holies." Yet, allowing our laments to flow as freely as our praise is no mean feat. Laments flow from grief and sorrow, which themselves come out of loss, disaster, and tragedy. Dombkowski Hopkins adds that "it takes courage to grieve honestly. The lament takes seriously our uncertainty about God when we are in the pit. It is our response to God's hiddenness that articulates that experience of hiddenness and brings it to speech. . . . The lament uncovers real doubt that emerges from the imbalance between the promises of God and the present situation."[6] Lament comes from the very moments in life when we may feel most disoriented, when our legs are the shakiest, when our heart is the most unsure. Too often, in a church built on statements of certainty, the uncertainty that necessarily emerges from the seeming imbalance between promised blessings and a current challenge can become a source of shame. Something that we bury deep within ourselves. When one is surrounded by the chorus of praises confidently claiming "I know . . ." then the laments of "O God, where are you . . ." can seem, somehow, out of place.

SILENCING LAMENT

When faced with those who need to lament, sometimes out of our own sense of discomfort with the evocative and provocative language of lament, we seek to prevent its expression. As Dombkowski Hopkins notes, in situations where we are face-to-face with those who need to lament, "well-meaning people . . . point to passages in the Bible [or to other books in the standard works] that talk about rock-solid faith that never waivers."[7] The implied message, it seems to me, is, "If these people can get through it so can you."

However, Dombkowski Hopkins suggests that such tactics often miss the mark: "This only proves that [well-meaning people] know their [scriptures] better than the human condition."[8] Much like Job's friends who eventually blamed Job for his suffering and chastised him for the boldness with which he challenged his situation (see Job 30:20–31), we, too often, muzzle those who might be on the precipice of honestly lamenting their condition because it does not match our modern notions of "proper" worship.

It seems to me that fear may be at the root of our hesitancy to allow those suffering from loss, disaster, and tragedy to worship through the language of lament. My sense is that this is because lament is not often modeled in our worship services and because we have not been taught to "hear the worship" embedded in lament. We are simply unable to see the profound covenantal clinging that accompanies language like this:

> *Save me, O God,*
> > *for the waters have come up to my neck.*
> *I sink in deep mire,*
> > *where there is no foothold. . . .*
> *My eyes grow dim*
> > *with waiting for my God.*
>
> > > (PSALM 69:1–3, NRSV)

In moments of disorientation, sorrow, or grief, what individuals may need most is the ability to express, without filter or reservation, those feelings to the One who is at the center of it all. And though that may be what they need, such opportunity is not given very often.

Lament can make those who hear it (fellow worshippers) uncomfortable. And because it creates discomfort it is silenced in a variety of ways, many of which seem innocuous, but which adds hurt upon hurt to those who are in pain. For instance, sometimes discomfort is communicated with downcast eyes, shifting feet, wringing hands, or whispers to a neighbor. These signals—however subtle—clearly suggest to the one speaking that such language should stay unspoken. Sometimes, when someone dares voice lament, our discomfort is manifested by quickly (and immediately) "correcting" the lamenter's expression of pain with language like, "Well, you may feel that way now, but I know . . ." Even if done without malice, when that approach is used we implicitly suggest to everyone that even in moments of disorientation and sorrow and grief, praise is *still* the only acceptable language and that expressions of lament should be excised or at least be quickly caveated with more comforting and familiar rhetoric. Or, we seek to remedy our discomfort by blithely dismissing their experience and covering it with the fig leaf of unrecognized blessing: "Everything happens for a reason!" "God is in control!" "This is a blessing in disguise!" When we react in any of these ways, we unintentionally hurt those who are already suffering.

The feelings of shame and faithlessness that arise from others' discomfort with lament language comes, I believe, from living in a Christian culture that places the highest value on a praise-focused approach to worship. We are steeped in a culture that fears the absence of praise. Lament is hard to hear. And so, rather than allowing space for lament so that those in pain can express their disorientation—to honestly, courageously, and authentically worship God through complaint—we too often bring shame instead of support to those who are hurting. This is a travesty of our own making, and it is inconsistent with Christianity's spiritual heritage.

LAMENT AND FIERCE COMMITMENT

The language of lament is one of the most powerful tools that Christians generally and Latter-day Saints specifically inherited from Israel's sacred traditions. As Brueggemann explains, laments "are not religious in the sense that they are courteous or polite or deferential . . . [but rather because] they are willing to articulate this chaos to the very face of the Holy One."[9] Relatedly, Dombkowski Hopkins notes, "The psalmists risk encounter in order to keep up relationship with God. There is no false reticence in Israelite piety. The psalmists dare to speak to God directly and honestly . . . to be angry with God is not impious, but an acknowledgement that God matters to us."[10] Church leaders have described this kind of boldness using phrases such as "sincere," "honest," "consecrated," and "striving" communication.[11] Israel believed in a God with whom they had unquestioned and unshakeable covenant; a God who valued relationship over pretense; a God who, even if intervention was not imminent, was present in its struggles; a God who listened; a God who understood that the act of complaint was an act of worship. Rather than lament signaling a frayed relationship with Deity, Israel's sacred tradition of lament indicates the fierceness with which Israel held onto the covenant. In fact, as noted earlier, these moments of our greatest vulnerability—our moments of fear, pain, anguish—are among the most holy we will ever have because those are the moments that draw us to God most unabashedly. When grief sets in, we become willing to kick open heaven's gates and demand answers. This is something we should embrace.

How can this be the case? How can complaining to God (and blaming God, as happens in some of the laments) demonstrate a fierce commitment to covenant? Isn't complaint an act of faithlessness or even betrayal? Far from faithlessness and betrayal, a remarkable feature of lament is that through the process of lament, the one who laments doubles down on the existence of God and the reality of a covenant relationship by taking their heaviest burdens—pain, anguish, and sorrow—directly to the source of all life: God. Though speaking about Psalm 32 specifically, Brueggemann's observation holds true for laments more generally: "There is no doubt here [in laments] about the reality of God."[12] Even when the language is stronger than that with which we may be comfortable, it is language that presumes (1) the existence of God, (2) faith in that God, (3) the belief that God cares, and (4) the expectation of covenant keeping on God's part. Seen this way, lament is as faithful a mode of worship as any strain of praise we might raise. As a case in point, let us look at Psalm 88, which, as was noted earlier, is the only lament in the Psalter in which there is no "turn." I chose this one *precisely because* of its *lack* of a turn. Can even a lament such as this be faithful and worshipful?

To begin, let us look at the psalm itself. I am including the entire psalm and removing the verse numbers so the poetry of the language is uninterrupted:

O Lord, God of my salvation,
    when, at night, I cry out in your presence,
let my prayer come before you;
incline your ear to my cry.

For my soul is full of troubles,
    and my life draws near to Sheol.
I am counted among those who go down to the Pit;
    I am like those who have no help,
like those forsaken among the dead,
    like the slain that lie in the grave,
like those whom you remember no more,

for they are cut off from your hand.
You have put me in the depths of the Pit,
 in the regions dark and deep.
Your wrath lies heavy upon me,
 and you overwhelm me with all your waves. . . .

You have caused my companions to shun me;
 you have made me a thing of horror to them.
I am shut in so that I cannot escape;
 my eye grows dim through sorrow.
Every day I call on you, O Lord;
 I spread out my hands to you.
Do you work wonders for the dead?
 Do the shades [ghosts] rise up to praise you? . . .
Is your steadfast love declared in the grave,
 or your faithfulness in Abaddon [a place of destruction]?
Are your wonders known in the darkness,
 or your saving help in the land of forgetfulness?

But I, O Lord, cry out to you;
 in the morning my prayer comes before you.
O Lord, why do you cast me off?
 Why do you hide your face from me?
Wretched and close to death from my youth up,
 I suffer your terrors; I am desperate.
Your wrath has swept over me;
 your dread assaults destroy me.
They surround me like a flood all day long;
 from all sides they close in on me.
You have caused friend and neighbor to shun me;
 my companions are in darkness.

(Psalm 88, NRSV)

This is a section of scripture that is rarely quoted in talks or firesides. It is scandalous language. In a praise-focused community, such language borders on embarrassing. Yet, it is scripture. And if there was ever a voice of pain, sorrow, and grief, Psalm 88 is it. We do not know what loss, disaster, or tragedy precipitated this lament, but we do not need to—the pain that is expressed herein is enough. And though some who read this psalm may never have felt these feelings, there are others who know *exactly* how this psalmist feels. This is bold and visceral language. How is this faithful worship? Returning to the four points I noted earlier as a framework for briefly analyzing this psalm will make its worshipful nature evident:

1. *Presumes the existence of God*—The lament is addressed to the "God of my salvation" and the psalmist uses the appellation "O Lord"— the English word used to represent the sacred name of God, YHWH—four different times. God's existence is unquestioned. God is being addressed directly and frequently.

2. *Presumes faith in that God*—The fact that the psalmist is speaking this *to* God is based on a faith *in* God. Presumably, one could accept the idea of God but lack faith in that God—however, such an approach is not likely to lead to prayer. A prayer like what we see in this psalm certainly would not be possible. In this instance we have not only prayer but intense supplication. This kind of supplication can only be premised on faith in the one to whom the prayer is addressed. Further, the psalmist implies that this is not the psalmist's first prayer. In the opening lines of the first and last stanza, the psalmist notes expressly that God is petitioned in prayer "at night" and "in the morning," and in the middle of the psalm the psalmist says that prayer occurs "every day." Taken together, these references seem to function as a literary device that likely indicates the

psalmist prays constantly. Again, this kind of persistence only makes sense in the context of faith.

3. *The belief that God cares*—As the psalmist chronicles the challenges being faced (close to death, desperation, no friends), there is no question whether or not God cares; the only question is one of timing—*when* will God intervene? In fact, the obvious confusion over the psalmist's situation that is voiced in the psalm comes from a place that presumes God has an interest in the psalmist's life. Said more directly, the psalmist's *presumption* of God's caring is the basis for the disorientation the psalmist feels.

4. *The expectation of covenant keeping on God's part*—In the third stanza, the psalmist asks a series of rhetorical questions challenging God to act like God. The psalmist observes that God's miracles make little sense for those who are already dead, where destruction has already occurred, and in places where people have already forgotten about God. The implication is that God should be acting on behalf of those still alive, before destruction occurs, and prior to forgetfulness. That is to say: with the backdrop of stories like the Passover and the Exodus from Egypt (of which the psalmist is no doubt aware), these rhetorical questions carry with them the *expectation* that God will act in covenantal ways on behalf of the petitioner, eventually.

To be sure, the psalm uses language that is raw and pain-filled, unfiltered and bold. The psalmist is daring. The psalmist is engaged in a risky faith that favors honesty over false piety and authenticity over appearances. As Brueggemann notes, "The unanswered plea does not silence the speaker.... The failure of God to respond does not lead to atheism or doubt in God. *It leads to more intense address.* This psalm, like faith of Israel, is utterly contained in the notion that Yahweh is there and must be addressed."[13] Make no mistake about it: in the act of lament, the psalmist is engaged in intense worship. This is a spiritual heritage for which we need to make more room.

Church members have been expressly taught by Elder Neal A. Maxwell to have faith in the One who "having 'descended below all things' . . . comprehends, perfectly and personally, the full range of human suffering."[14] This builds on Israel's ancient foundations of belief in a God who "is present in, participating in, and attentive to the darkness, weakness, and displacement of life."[15] In other words, because God understands the full range of human suffering, when we feel sorrow, grief, and pain, we know that we are not alone in that moment; God is, in fact, present *with us* in our sorrow, grief, and pain. Thus, by making room for lament, we also make room for a mode of worship that those who are suffering can use to approach God from within that pain. Worship does not require first overcoming life's challenges, let alone require feeling joyful and happy as a prelude to relationship. The God that Israel knows, the God that Nephi knows, and the God that Joseph Smith knows is a God who knows pain and is not afraid of an authentic covenant relationship, and all the messiness that surrounds such closeness. Worship is for the good times and the bad. Worship can happen on those Sundays when we make it to church with bells on our shoes and feel to sing songs of praise, and worship can happen on those Sundays when we come to church with a heart full of sorrow, and worship can happen even on those Sundays when life is so hard we are unsure if we can get out of bed at all. Our spiritual heritage is one of a God who is as open to songs of praise as to songs of lament. God is strong enough to be our God in all seasons of our life.

CHAPTER 4

FINDING OUR VOICE THROUGH LAMENT

BREAKING THE SILENCE

Loss, disaster, and tragedy can lead to silence. In fact, Elder Jeffrey R. Holland observes, "Some of the world's most painful suffering is done in silence."[1] There are many reasons for this. In some instances, the loss, disaster, and tragedy feel too big for language. The *Shoah*[2] (one Hebrew word for the Holocaust), or the Rwandan, Bosnian, or Armenian genocides, or the slave trade or sex trafficking, or the eradication of native peoples and their cultures across the globe, or the use of nuclear weapons on Hiroshima and Nagasaki, or starvation and disease, and so many other human tragedies are all so profoundly horrific that the words to express the grief, sorrow, and sadness that these events elicit may not be readily available. Or, in some instances, the loss, disaster, and tragedy are too personal for language; the death of a child or spouse, or the loss of our faith community, or a betrayal from someone we trusted. These may cut so close to the heart that trying to find words of grief, sorrow, and sadness could further strain the few, thin threads holding our life together in the wake of such a tragedy. In some instances the cut is so deep and so damaging that our mind tries to block our memories of those events altogether, such as instances of serious abuse or the trauma of war. Our body tries to silence the pain as a means of protection. Maybe even in most instances, and in a way that is as banal as it is terrible, we are simply ashamed of how we feel. Shame keeps us quiet.

It is precisely because loss, disaster, and tragedy can lead to silence that we need to make room for lament. In a praise-focused approach to worship, the language of sadness, grief, and sorrow, if it is allowed at all, is muted and suppressed. When only praise can be spoken, those who cannot echo that praise may say nothing at all. And for those buried under the burden of grief and despair, attending a praise-focused worship service can be doubly painful. Michael Card described this situation with great deftness. He says that as a body of believers, we "lack the language to describe our desolate place in this frustratingly verdant [i.e., lush, fertile] place. Bound by the personal sorrow and hurts we leave outside the door on a thousand Sundays, we are left to languish while those around us drink from a fountain that, to our eyes, looks dry . . . we find ourselves unable to speak. We are word-less."[3] We hear the refrains of praise, but they do not speak to our heart. We see others being fed, but we feel a gnawing pang in our bellies. We listen to stories of God's abundance but perceive only destruction around us. We want to cry with anguish but allow no words of sorrow to cross our lips. The apparent greenness of the "church garden" feels like an accusation when our "personal gardens" are barren. This is why we need to make space for lament.

Lament is one way to break the silence that often accompanies loss, disaster, and tragedy. And often, breaking the silence is the first step toward healing. Lament can help us break the silence in at least two ways. First, we may be able to use our own voice to worship through lament. It could be that, in defiance of the silence that accompanies loss, disaster, and tragedy, we are able to find enough language to raise a voice of complaint to God in faithful worship. When this is possible, we can find reservoirs of strength in approaching God in our moments of greatest weakness. However, this is not always possible. So, second, in those moments when the loss, disaster, and tragedy lead to a seemingly unbreakable silence, we can locate ourselves in language that is already present in sacred text. By "finding ourselves" in these scriptural texts, and then letting those texts, including laments, speak *for us* until we are able to find our own voice, we create room for ourselves to build our own strength and resolve. Each of these approaches has scriptural precedent. Let me treat them one at a time and then offer some reflections on both.

SPEAKING IN YOUR OWN VOICE: JEREMIAH

Jeremiah was the prophet in Jerusalem when Jerusalem fell to the Babylonian empire. According to tradition, the Old Testament writings known as Lamentations are attributed to the prophet Jeremiah's reaction to witnessing this event. As noted earlier, in Hebrew this collection of poetic laments is titled simply *'Ekhah,* which translates to "How, or Alas." But before we can truly appreciate Lamentations, Jeremiah's story needs to be reviewed.

According to the text, Jeremiah began his ministry to Judah in the "thirteenth year of [King] Josiah," or about 627 BCE (Jeremiah 25:3), and he remained prophet through the rest of Josiah's reign as well as through the rule of Jehoahaz, Jehoiakim, Jehoiachin, and Zedekiah. He was from the town of Anathoth and so potentially belonged to the priestly family of Abiathar. In the days of Solomon (hundreds of years before Jeremiah's time), Abiathar, who was a powerful priest in Jerusalem, had supported Solomon's rival's claim to the throne. Upon replacing David as king of Israel, Solomon decided to exile Abiathar back to Anathoth instead of killing him like he had done with the others who threatened his place on the throne. Solomon sent Abiathar "unto thine own fields" (1 Kings 2:26) and promoted the priestly family of Zadock who had, alongside Nathan, supported his ascension (see 1 Kings 1–2). Jeremiah's familial connection to the priests of Anathoth suggests that Jeremiah was, thus, from a family who had spent generations in exile, and therefore there is reason to believe that that Jeremiah may have been seen as an outsider by the powerful and well-connected of Jerusalem. Jeremiah may have also had a chip on his shoulder.

By all accounts, Jeremiah was an enigmatic and not particularly well-liked prophetic figure who was known for public displays that enacted the message he taught: burying his underwear by the Euphrates, then unearthing the same (now-ruined) garment to show how the pride of Jerusalem will also be ruined (see Jeremiah 13); smashing jars of human excrement to demonstrate how God will bring disaster on the people of Jerusalem (see Jeremiah 19); and putting himself in a yoke to show how the people of Jerusalem will be brought into bondage (see Jeremiah 27). As such public displays might suggest, Jeremiah's message about the greed and lack of covenant fidelity on the part of those in Jerusalem was as direct as it was forceful (see, for instance, Jeremiah 6:13–15; 7:1–21). Further, I imagine those whom he castigated did not appreciate the creative ways in which Jeremiah delivered his message. In a show of boldness, Jeremiah warned King Zedekiah that if Judah did not willingly surrender to Babylon, then Jerusalem would be destroyed (see Jeremiah 27:5–11). This message was not well-received, and Jeremiah was first thrown into a cistern and then, after he escaped, imprisoned. He stayed imprisoned until Jerusalem fell to Babylon (see Jeremiah 38).

The Babylonian conquest of Judah happened over the course of about a decade. In 597 BCE, Nebuchadnezzar's army overwhelmed Jerusalem's forces, and Nebuchadnezzar removed the "treasures" from the temple—the epicenter of worship and the symbol of God's presence among God's people. Then his forces deported to Babylon "all the princes, and all the mighty men of valour, . . . and all the craftsmen and smiths," leaving only "the poorest" people behind (2 Kings 24:14). Incidentally, Ezekiel, who would later raise a prophetic voice to the Israelites while in Babylonian exile, was likely part of this first deportation, a signal of his social prominence in Jerusalem. Then, in about 586 BCE, Nebuzaradan, Nebuchadnezzar's captain of the guard, completed the destruction of Jerusalem by dismantling its walls, burning all the homes to the ground, destroying the king's palace, and razing the temple. He also deported what social elite remained, again leaving behind "the poor of the land to be vinedressers and husbandmen" (2 Kings 25:12). Jeremiah was eventually released from prison by the Babylonian invaders and given the choice to go "whither it seemeth good and convenient for thee to go." Jeremiah chose to live among the people that remained "in the land" (Jeremiah 40:4, 6). However, even that did not last, and Jeremiah was eventually forced to flee to Egypt and likely died there (see Jeremiah 43).

As is evident by the brief recounting of his history, Jeremiah lived a life marked by loss, disaster, and tragedy. He was disliked by those he tried to serve. His prophetic warning was ignored. He was left to die in a cistern and then thrown in prison. And, unlike the rich and powerful who were taken to Babylon, who heard about but did not see the destruction of Jerusalem, Jeremiah actually saw the carnage that was left by the armies of Babylon. He was a firsthand witness to the death and devastation in Jerusalem. Perhaps he stood at the gates of what used to be the temple of God but was now a pile of rubble; perhaps he cried with the poor who had not been "important enough" to deport but whose entire lives had been destroyed. We do not know for certain what he saw, but we can infer from his writings that whatever it was, it affected him deeply. Eventually, Jeremiah died in exile. Though Jeremiah's name means something like "Yah[weh] will exalt/uplift," it is not hard to see why Jeremiah is also known as "the weeping prophet."

Jeremiah's reaction to seeing Jerusalem destroyed, as recorded in Lamentations, is emotionally searing.[4] To get a sense of what Lamentations expresses, I have selected portions from the text as illustrative, but the whole collection is relatively short. For those who have the desire, it is worth reading Lamentations in its entirety.

Behold, and see
If there be any sorrow like unto my sorrow,
Which is done unto me,
Wherewith the Lord hath afflicted me
In the day of his fierce anger. . . .
He hath made me desolate
And faint all the day.

(Lamentations 1:12–13)

Behold, O Lord; for I am in distress:
My bowels are troubled; . . .
All mine enemies have heard of my trouble;
They are glad that thou hast done it. . . .
For my sighs are many,
And my heart is faint.

(Lamentations 1:20–22)

The Lord hath swallowed up all the habitations of Jacob,
And hath not pitied:
He hath thrown down in his wrath
The strong holds of the daughter of Judah. . . .
The Lord was as an enemy:
He hath swallowed up Israel. . . .
He hath destroyed his places of the assembly:
The Lord hath caused the solemn feasts and sabbaths to be
    forgotten in Zion. . . .
Mine eyes do fail with tears,
My bowels are troubled,
My liver is poured upon the earth,
For the destruction of the daughter of my people.

(Lamentations 2:2, 5–6, 11)

[The Lord] hath also broken my teeth with gravel stones,
He hath covered me with ashes.
And thou hast removed my soul far off from peace:
I forgat prosperity.

(LAMENTATIONS 3:16–17)

Mine eye runneth down with rivers of water
For the destruction of the daughter of my people.
Mine eye trickleth down, and ceaseth not,
Without any intermission. . . .
I said, I am cut off.
I called upon thy name, O LORD,
Out of the low dungeon. . . .
Hide not thine ear at my breathing, at my cry.

(LAMENTATIONS 3:48–49, 54–56)

Remember, O LORD, what is come upon us:
Consider, and behold our reproach.
We are orphans and fatherless,
Our mothers are as widows.
Our necks are under persecution:
We labour, and have no rest.
The joy of our heart is ceased;
Our dance is turned into mourning.
Wherefore dost thou forget us for ever,
And forsake us so long time?

(LAMENTATIONS 5:1, 3, 5, 15, 20)

The book of Lamentations is five chapters of heart-wrenching, poetic expressions of sorrow and grief. In the face of the loss, disaster, and tragedy Jeremiah experienced, faithful worship required the language of lament. In this moment—as witness to the annihilation of all he knew and loved and upon seeing the wreckage of the city as it lay smoldering before him—without lament, there may have been nothing to say. Silence may have reigned supreme. Yes, this lament is stark and, at times, haunting. But this is what the voice of grief and sorrow sounds like. God does not silence this language, and neither should we. In Lamentations we hear the voice of one who is in pain but who has also found a way to bring the complaint to God in an authentic way. And, I hope, at this point it is clear that there is nothing faithless about Jeremiah's language of despair.

Even with the stark language used in Lamentations, there is no doubt about God's existence, nor is there a lack of faith in that God. In this language, we have a model of what it means to have *faith enough* to take sorrow and grief directly to the footstool of God with the expectation that God will listen, hear, care, and engage in a covenantal relationship. Jeremiah's laments are *the language of worship* in the midst of devastation. Even today, Jewish communities read Lamentations in its entirety on the Ninth of Av, a day of fast during which they mourn the destruction of the temples (by the Babylonians in 586 BCE, and the second temple by the Romans in 70 CE). And selections from Lamentations are also included in the readings surrounding Lent for Christian denominations that follow the liturgical calendar. There is a time to mourn—the inclusion of Lamentations in our sacred text, and its continued use today, makes that clear.

SPEAKING IN YOUR OWN VOICE: JOSEPH SMITH

In some ways, we see echoes of Jeremiah's situation in Joseph Smith's life and in his letter from Liberty Jail, portions of which are found in Doctrine and Covenants 121. Because of a deeper familiarity among the Latter-day Saint community with Joseph's story than with Jeremiah's, it is sufficient to say that Joseph came from a meager background, he was often dismissed or ignored by those in power, his efforts to bring about the promised Restoration were met with struggles around every corner, he was disliked by many outside (and some inside) his community, the Saints had been forced to abandon settlement after settlement (which included leaving behind the Kirtland Temple), and he had spent a significant amount of time in prison. By March of 1839, after a lifetime of persecution, numerous legal challenges, many months of incarceration, and knowing of the persecution being faced by others whom he loved, Joseph may have felt a little like Jeremiah. Upon reflection on all of this, as he sat in prison, Joseph penned these words of lament:

> *O God, where art thou? And where is the pavilion that covereth thy hiding place?*
> *How long shall thy hand be stayed, and thine eye, yea thy pure eye, behold from the eternal heavens the wrongs of thy people and of thy servants, and thine ear be penetrated with their cries?*
> *Yea, O Lord, how long shall they suffer these wrongs and unlawful oppressions, before thine heart shall be softened toward them, and thy bowels be moved with compassion toward them?*
>
> *O Lord God Almighty, maker of heaven, earth, and seas, and of all things that in them are, and who controllest and subjectest the devil, and the dark and benighted dominion of Sheol—*
> *stretch forth thy hand; let thine eye pierce; let thy pavilion be taken up;*
> *let thy hiding place no longer be covered; let thine ear be inclined;*
> *let thine heart be softened,*
> *and thy bowels moved with compassion toward us.*
> *Let thine anger be kindled against our enemies;*

*and, in the fury of thine heart, with thy sword avenge us of
our wrongs.*

*Remember thy suffering saints, O our God;
    and thy servants will rejoice in thy name forever.*
                                                    (D&C 121:1–6)

As is the case with Lamentations, there is nothing faithless about this language. There is no doubt about God's existence, nor is there a lack of faith in that God. In this language, as with Lamentations, we have a model of what it means to have *faith enough* to take sorrow and grief directly to the footstool of God with the expectation that God will listen, hear, care, and engage in a covenant relationship. This is the language of worship. In this text, as with Lamentations, Joseph's lament is a protest. But it is not a protest against God—*it is a protest against silence*. Like Jeremiah, in taking their complaint to God, Joseph and the many others who have lamented have undertaken a holy protest against the shame, fear, and loss of relationship. They are speaking even when embroiled in the kinds of sorrow and grief that threaten to stop the voice of worship altogether.

LETTING SACRED TEXT SPEAK FOR US: HANNAH

But sometimes, the moment is too big, too personal, or too deep. Sometimes we cannot find our own voice, not even in the language of lament. If lament is a protest against silence, what happens when we lack even the ability to speak a lament? Does silence win? It is in these moments, when we may not feel we have a voice, that the language of sacred text can help us find our footing. When we do not have the ability to voice our own lament, we can deploy the language of scripture on our behalf. The language of scripture—such as the psalms of lament—can *become* our voice until either our sentiments have been fully expressed or we find strength enough to speak with our own voice.

Amy-Jill Levine and Marc Zvi Brettler make the case that the Old Testament's recounting of Hannah's prayers surrounding the birth of her son Samuel (1 Samuel 1–2) suggest this is exactly how psalms were deployed in the "real life" of those who believed in and worshipped the God of Abraham, Isaac, and Jacob. Individuals have always retained the ability to pass their supplication to God in whatever way seemed fitting—the scriptures are replete with individual prayers. But Levine and Brettler point to Hannah as emblematic of how individuals, when faced with "extreme situations, whether dire or thankful," looked to more "formal poetic prayers" (i.e., psalms, such as laments) as a tool of supplication.[5] Thus, Hannah's story is illustrative for this discussion.

We first learn of Hannah when she comes to the tabernacle at Shiloh to petition God for a child—the tabernacle had been erected at Shiloh very soon after the Israelites' arrival in Canaan (see Joshua 1:18) and was a center of Israel's worship until the temple was finally built in Jerusalem. Levine and Brettler observe that Hannah's prayer at the tabernacle is simple, personal, and direct.[6] However, and importantly for this conversation, Hannah's prayer is unspoken—she says nothing out loud (which becomes important in her story, as we shall see). She is, to the eyes and ears of all around her, silent. In her silent prayer, she vows that if God will allow her to have a son, then she "will set him before [the Lord] as a nazirite until the day of his death" (1 Samuel 1:11, NRSV). The priest at Shiloh, Eli, thought she was drunk because she was moving her lips but not making any noise, and chastised her: "How long will you make a drunken spectacle of yourself? Put away your wine" (1 Samuel 1:14, NRSV). But Hannah protested the false charge, and Eli, realizing his error, offered her a blessing: "Go in peace; the God of Israel grant the petition you have made to him" (1 Samuel 1:17, NRSV). The next morning, she conceived. Hannah raised Samuel until "she weaned him" (1 Samuel 1:23) and then, consistent with her vow, brought the child and an offering (a bull, an ephah of flour, and some wine) back to the tabernacle at Shiloh to turn over her firstborn child to Eli to be raised by the priest. It is at this point that Hannah deployed a psalm.

With that basic story in mind, it is worth slowing down for a moment to look at Hannah's life a little more closely. As the story opens, Hannah approaches the tabernacle in Shiloh, on her own, to petition God for a gift. Hannah was the second wife of a man named Elkanah; the other wife, Peninnah, had children, but Hannah did not (see 1 Samuel 1:2). Like Sarah, Rebekah, and Rachel before her, Hannah is a barren woman in a society where barrenness carried negative social and religious reverberations.[7] Further, the text records that Peninnah, referred to as Hannah's "rival," would "provoke her severely" (1 Samuel 1:6) because of her childlessness. Though Hannah's husband did not seem to be bothered by her barrenness, it was a source of pain for Hannah. In fact, the scriptures record that "Hannah wept and would not eat" (1 Samuel 1:7, NRSV) because of her predicament. In the twenty-first century, we can recognize that she was likely suffering from depression. This description of her, when considered with the image of Hannah at the tabernacle bargaining with God, indicates that Hannah was emotionally and physically worn down. She was desperate for a child. Anyone who has struggled with infertility or other challenges in which the pangs of life cut so deep as to be almost all-consuming will likely be able to commiserate with how Hannah may have felt. Whether it is a desire to find a spouse, hope that a loved one will recover from a medical procedure or illness, wanting a family rift to be healed, finding a runaway child, overcoming challenges with addiction, struggling to secure the basic necessities of life for oneself and family, or any of the myriad life experiences that are faced by us and our neighbors, we have all at some point been at the end of our rope, when weeping comes without warning and everyday tasks become a chore, and the only thing left to do is bargain with God.

What's more, it is interesting, though not terribly surprising, that Hannah—even in the act of bargaining with God—is voiceless. The words of her prayer, which she apparently uttered in her heart and mind, never cross her lips. *She. Is. Silent.* Perhaps this was because she was embarrassed to be bargaining with God? Perhaps she did not feel worthy to be praying at the tabernacle because of her barrenness? Perhaps it was the years of exhaustion at her situation (in the scriptures it says she suffered "year by year" [1 Samuel 1:7].) Perhaps there were other people close by, and her prayer was too personal to be voiced within earshot of others? Perhaps it was that, in this moment, she simply lacked the strength to form words? All we know is that Hannah describes herself as having "great anxiety and vexation" (1 Samuel 1:17, NRSV) and that even when questioned by the priest Eli about what she was doing, Hannah does not reveal her purpose. The scriptures do not explain why Hannah could not pray out loud, but I have seen in my own life and observed in the lives of others that it is often in the times of our sorest trials, in moments of our most personal struggles, that we find ourselves unable to give voice to the deepest desires of our heart. It is when we need speech the most that it fails us. Parenthetically, it is worth reflecting on whether we sometimes misjudge others of the human family because they appear metaphorically drunk, when in reality their hearts are so heavy that they simply lack the language to speak their truth.

As Hannah's story develops, the emotional milieu becomes even more complex. Against all odds, after Eli's nonspecific blessing, she is able to conceive and gives birth to a son: Samuel. In the Old Testament, Samuel would end up playing a critical role. He begins Israel's "prophetic" tradition.[8] He is the prophet that witnesses the first stages of development of the Kingdom of Israel under the leadership of Saul. And he anoints Saul (at the people's request) to be their first king (something he warns against; see 1 Samuel 8–10), which sets the stage for the coming of King David. However, at the time of his birth, Samuel was simply a mother's child. A baby. It is hard to imagine the mix of emotions that Hannah must have felt when Samuel was born. Certainly, overwhelming exultation and joy. But, knowing that she had made a vow to "give" him to the Lord (1 Samuel 1:11), it is easy to believe that exultation and joy was tinged with sadness and melancholy. She would likely not see him grow up; she would miss major milestones in his life. Samuel was her baby for now . . . but eventually she would entrust his life into someone else's care. It is perhaps only those who have had the courage to place a child for adoption who can truly empathize with the mix of emotions Hannah might have felt.

But Hannah did as she vowed she would do. She cared for and raised the child until he was old enough that he could be safely entrusted to Eli. It is unclear how old Samuel might have been when he left his childhood home for the last time—all the scriptures say is that "the child was young" (1 Samuel 1:24). But I am confident that no matter how old he was, Hannah likely felt that she had not had enough time with her son. Still, in a remarkable demonstration of commitment and faith, she takes the boy back to the tabernacle and says to Eli: "I am the woman who was standing here in your presence, praying to the LORD. For this child I prayed; and the LORD has granted me the petition that I made to him. Therefore I have lent him to the LORD; as long as he lives, he is given to the LORD" (1 Samuel 1:26–28, NRSV). Her words must have cracked with emotion. And then the scriptures say simply, "She left [Samuel] there" (1 Samuel 1:28, NRSV). My heart breaks when I try to imagine how Hannah must have felt.

Then Hannah prays out loud. This prayer is recorded in 1 Samuel 2:1–10. Though the text does not say this explicitly, the fact that the language of the prayer is in a stylized format—a clearly poetic and stylized statement of faith—makes me think that the prayer was spoken aloud, perhaps in the process of a formal worship process.[9] Given that she could not find a voice to speak her petition *before* Samuel's conception, I find it doubly remarkable that Hannah is able to find a way to pray *after* she entrusts Samuel to Eli and witnesses her son and the priest disappear into the sanctuary. And how does she do this? The language she uses, which is quite formal both in tone and structure, suggests Hannah uses a psalm that was not of her creation but was instead a psalm that was contemporaneously available and part of her worship tradition. It is worth noticing that Hannah uses a psalm of thanksgiving to find her voice. We will talk more about "the turn" in chapter 6, but apparently Hannah was able to move from anxiety, exhaustion, weeping, and silence and into newness. Interestingly, Brueggemann affirms that thanksgiving and lament are intimately related: "The song of thanksgiving is in fact the lament restated after the crisis has been dealt with."[10] In her turn from lament to praise, Hannah "located herself" within the liturgical language of her community. Levine and Brettler affirm that psalms were "part of the Levite's repertoire" and could be "reused, perhaps with modifications, by other worshipers."[11] In this instance, it seems, Hannah reached into her religious tradition and used the language of a preexisting psalm to find her voice.

Psalms, including lament psalms, act as a tool of supplication for those in extreme situations. In essence, rather than struggling to find the words for oneself—a task that is nigh impossible in moments of emotional turmoil—someone can simply allow the words of scripture to give a voice to the voiceless. And if there were ever an example of an extreme situation, Hannah's qualifies. In this moment, as she handed over her much longed-for son to be raised by someone else, Hannah leaned on the language of liturgy in order to have a voice. Or, said another way, preexisting liturgical language provided Hannah the means to locate herself emotionally in the worship practices of her people and gave her the ability to speak even when her own words may have failed her. Sacred text created the emotional space for her to voice her worship honestly. This is exactly how the lament language we find in the scriptures can function for all of us who have a hard time finding our voice when disaster comes.

LETTING SACRED TEXT SPEAK FOR US: JESUS

It is not hard to notice how Hannah's use of a psalm is similar to the way in which the Gospels of Matthew and Mark record Jesus's invoking of Psalm 22. As discussed earlier, the way in which Jesus uses the phrase "My God, my God, why hast thou forsaken me?" might speak to some of Jesus's feelings in that moment. Informed by the discussion of how Hannah used a thanksgiving psalm to find her voice, we can also now see how, in his moment of agony, Jesus let a lament psalm be his voice. Again, I want to be careful here, because I do not want anyone to think I am implying that Jesus lacked the ability in those final moments to find his voice. Rather, what I want to suggest is that (like Hannah), in a moment of emotional turmoil—his final moments on the cross—Jesus was able to locate himself within the scriptural tradition of his people and then use that scripture (specifically a psalm of lament) to speak *on his behalf*. However, what about the Gospels of Luke and John? Perhaps not surprisingly, those Gospels *also* record Jesus quoting psalms of laments (albeit different psalms) at the time of his death.

In the Gospel of Luke, Jesus is recorded as saying, "Father, into your hands I commend my spirit" (Luke 23:46, NRSV). This is a reference to Psalm 31:5, another of the Psalter's laments. As was likely the case with the Psalm 22 reference that is recorded in Mark and Matthew, Jesus's referencing of Psalm 31 in Luke shows Jesus locating himself within his sacred tradition and demonstrates the way that Jesus, in this moment of final grief, lets the lament speak *for him* and become *his voice*. Consider the power that Psalm 31 might carry when framed in the context of Jesus's Crucifixion:

> *In thee, O Lord, do I put my trust; let me never be ashamed: deliver me in thy righteousness.*
> *Bow down thine ear to me; deliver me speedily: be thou my strong rock, for an house of defence to save me.*
> *For thou art my rock and my fortress; therefore for thy name's sake lead me, and guide me.*
> *Pull me out of the net that they have laid privily for me: for thou art my strength.*
> *Into thine hand I commit my spirit: thou hast redeemed me, O Lord God of truth. . . .*
> *I will be glad and rejoice in thy mercy: for thou hast considered my trouble; thou hast known my soul in adversities. . . .*
> *Have mercy upon me, O Lord, for I am in trouble: mine eye is consumed with grief, yea, my soul and my belly.*
> *For my life is spent with grief. . . .*
> *I was a reproach among all mine enemies, but especially among my neighbours, and a fear to mine acquaintance: they that did see me without fled from me.*
> *I am forgotten as a dead man out of mind: I am like a broken vessel.*
> *For I have heard the slander of many: fear was on every side: while they took counsel together against me, they devised to take away my life.*
> *But I trusted in thee, O Lord: I said, Thou art my God. . . .*
> *O love the Lord, all ye his saints: for the Lord preserveth the faithful, and plentifully rewardeth the proud doer.*
> *Be of good courage, and he shall strengthen your heart, all ye that hope in the Lord.*
>
> (Psalm 31:1–5, 7, 9–14, 23–24).

We see a similar pattern in the Gospel of John. In John's Gospel, Jesus's penultimate words are, "I thirst" (John 19:28), which is an explicit reference to Psalm 69:21. Like Psalms 22 and 31, Psalm 69 is *also* a lament psalm (portions of this psalm were quoted in chapter 3, so I will not reprint them here, but they are worth reviewing again). And, as in the other Gospels, by invoking this psalm Jesus not only signals to us how he might have felt in this moment—when faced with the loss, disaster, and tragedy of the cross, which could have reasonably resulted in silence—but also establishes a model for us. Jesus, the strongest among us, showed that there is no weakness in leaning on scripture. Jesus was able to locate himself in sacred text and let that sacred text be his voice of lament.

THE VOICE OF LAMENT

Often one of the most disconcerting parts of loss, disaster, and tragedy is the sense of dislocation that the disorientation creates. We may not only feel unsure but also unmoored. In those moments, it can feel like being in a tilt-a-whirl, at a complete loss as to where we are. The very ground on which we are standing feels unfirm. In moments like this, it may feel nearly impossible to act, much less find our voice. But sacred text can help. Dombkowski Hopkins notes that "the ability to locate yourself in language, despite absolute powerlessness, can have a liberating effect because it ends the silence."[12] In some cases that may mean that we use our own language, as we saw with Jeremiah and Joseph. And in other cases, we can locate ourselves in the scriptures, as was modeled by Hannah and Jesus. But in either instance, voicing lament is an act of worship.

In whatever way we find a voice, we need not worry about whether our laments are sufficiently articulate or eloquent. God hears. President Russell M. Nelson encourages us to reach out to God with "the very longings of your heart."[13] God heard the "cry" of the Israelites suffering in the oppression of Pharaoh (Exodus 3:7). The word translated as "cry" in English is the Hebrew word *tseaqah*, which connotes a cry of distress that has been heard.[14] There is little reason to believe that this cry of distress was either articulate or eloquent, but God heard their cry, nonetheless. In fact, in the New Testament, Paul teaches that the Spirit can assist us as we seek to take our pain, sorrow, and grief to God. Paul says, "Likewise the Spirit also helpeth our infirmities: for we know not what we should pray for as we ought: but the Spirit itself maketh intercession for us with groanings which cannot be uttered" (Romans 8:26). Here the Greek word for "groaning" is *stenagmos*, which connotes a reaction brought on by enormous pressure.[15] Paul seems to be suggesting that when we are suffering under the loss, disaster, and tragedy of life—when we are freighted with the enormous pressure these kinds of events exert and we are so unmoored that we "know not what we should pray for" and we have nothing left but "groanings which cannot be uttered"—the Spirit will help ensure that our lament is heard. These verses make clear that lament, even inarticulate and ineloquent cries of distress and groanings, make their way to the very throne of God.

The validation of lament in our sacred tradition, and our sacred texts' recognition of lament as one of the ways in which we worship, calls for a reconsideration of any sense that praise-focused worship should be prioritized or privileged. As the Catholic theologian Gustavo Gutierrez explained, our scriptures make it exceptionally clear that "those who suffer unjustly have a right to complain and protest."[16] Brueggemann affirms this position: "There is nothing out of bounds, nothing precluded or inappropriate. Everything properly belongs in this conversation of the heart. To withhold parts of life from that conversation is in fact to withhold part of life from the sovereignty of God."[17] In fact, he suggests that "the absence of lament makes a religion of coercive obedience the only possibility."[18] I am not suggesting that a praise-focused approach is wrong—in fact, quite the contrary is true. Praise is an important part of worship. But I am suggesting that we need to intentionally struggle against the silence that sometimes accompanies sorrow, grief, and pain by making spaces in our communities for lament.

As Michael Card explains, "Lament expresses one of the most intimate moments of faith—not a denial of it. It is supreme honesty before a God whom my faith tells me I can trust."[19] If this is so, then those who suffer should be able to voice that complaint privately *and* in church. If we cannot bring to God the sorrow, grief, and pain we will inevitably feel through the voice of lament—privately and in public worship services—then our worship will reflect only an incomplete portion of the human experience. Excluding lament from our spiritual communities is like trying to play basketball with a team of individuals who all have one arm tied behind their backs. To take a little creative license with a well-known Joseph Smith statement, a religion that does not allow us to offer God every component of our human experience will never have the power sufficient to produce the faith necessary unto life and salvation.[20]

CHAPTER 5

USING LAMENT TO HOLD ON

VALIDATING, CLAIMING, AND WORSHIPPING FROM WITHIN OUR EXPERIENCE

Lament can be a lifeline when loss, disaster, and tragedy invade our experience. Lament's lifeline works in at least two different ways. First, the language of lament validates our lived experiences and then claims those experiences as sacred. There is sometimes a desire to "erase" loss, disaster, and tragedy by either minimizing painful experiences or by trying to reframe them as blessings. Seeing, really seeing, the suffering of others is difficult; it should not be surprising that we all tend to shy away. While this may sound problematic at best and heartless at worst, I believe it is most often well-meaning people who unintentionally try to "erase" loss through their attempts to offer support.

In her book *Everything Happens for a Reason and Other Lies I've Loved*, Kate Bowler includes an entire appendix of phrases good people use that may seem comforting on the surface but which in reality try to hide away (or erase) the loss, disaster, and tragedy of one who is suffering.[1] Phrases like "Well, at least . . ." or "It could be worse . . ." or "Don't forget that you still have . . ." or "See it as a blessing that . . ." or "When you get older you'll see . . ." may seem aimed at helping the person who is suffering, but in reality, the only thing they do is alleviate the discomfort of the one offering the advice. Your husband died? Well, at least . . . You lost your job? It could be worse . . . You were diagnosed with cancer? Don't forget you still have . . . When these phrases are laid out this starkly, I think it becomes clear that such phrases—by minimizing suffering or reframing it as a blessing—really only make *us* feel better when we say them. And once we feel better, the suffering of those around us is effectively expunged from our view, because we have minimized it or reframed it. Even worse, such language implicitly suggests that the victim, the one suffering, lacks faithfulness enough to see God's goodness for him/herself (since these phrases erase suffering and replace it with "unacknowledged blessings"). When we do this (and I have inadvertently done it, just as others probably have), we pile pain upon pain. And when suffering is successfully hidden by the veil of unacknowledged blessings, we do not have to think about uncomfortable ideas like why people suffer and, even more personally, the possibility that suffering may be heading our way eventually. The attempt to avoid the reality of grief and sorrow is one more way that we retreat back into a praise-focused approach to worship, covering our eyes and ears so that we no longer have to acknowledge that misery exists.

Lament rejects the tendency we all have to avoid confronting grief and sorrow, and in this way, lament can serve as a lifeline to those who are suffering. Lament "give[s] shape, power, visibility, authenticity to the experience."[2] Lament makes space for us to claim that painful experience, without excuse, justification, or a need to explain it away. Instead of minimizing pain, lament gives us room to express our pain. Instead of forcing upon grief and sorrow the cloak of "unrecognized blessing," lament allows us to simply express how we feel. Lament pushes back on the momentum to silence, dismiss, or ignore suffering. Lament gives a way for those who are in the pit, and who are troubled on every side, to *acknowledge* and *claim* suffering as part of one's lived experience.

Second, lament gives us a way to worship, i.e., to stay in relationship with God, even when praise is not forthcoming. Lament does not require that the grief, sorrow, and sadness depart before worship can begin, but rather lament is the vehicle that allows us to worship from within our suffering. For those of us who have spent time crushed under the weight of sorrow, and who felt like others refused to see our pain or hear our sorrow, lament reminds us that our pain and sorrow, voiced authentically and honestly, are seen and heard by God. When the language of praise is, for a time, unspeakable, the lifeline of lament reminds us that cries of sorrow and grief are just as sacred. And because lament treats our grief and sadness as sacred, these feelings of grief and sadness can now become the basis from which we worship.

Too often the word *sacred* is used to imply something that is deeply personal or not for disclosure, or revealed by God to only a select few. The word *sacred* is sometimes a shorthand way to describe a precipice of insight that follows, or is based upon, acts of righteousness or the result of worthiness and that is not for public consumption. That is to say, sometimes we seem to suggest that it is because we act righteously or live worthily we are able to have not-for-sharing experiences that others cannot have, and that those experiences are, therefore, *sacred*. Consider the way the temple is sometimes discussed: because we are deemed to be righteous/worthy, we can attend the temple to participate in rituals that are sacred (deeply personal, not for disclosure, revealed by God only to those who are selected to participate). Thus, the temple is a *sacred* place. This colloquial use of the word *sacred* in the worship tradition of Latter-day Saints—as compared against the traditions Latter-day Saints inherited from ancient Israel—is incomplete and potentially misleading. Within the worship tradition of Israel, the word *sacred* simply connotes something that has been consecrated for God.[3] Its opposite is not *unrighteous*, *evil*, or *widely known*, but simply *unconsecrated*. In ancient Israel, the animal sacrifice taken to the temple—the part that was for God—was sacred; the other animals that remained in their pens were unconsecrated. Neither animal was more worthy nor more valued than the other; rather, one was for God and one was not—that was the only difference. Again, the grain offered as part of Israel's temple worship was sacred; the rest of the grain was unconsecrated. Neither bushel was intrinsically superior to the other; rather, one was for God and one was not. That expanded understanding of the word *sacred*, when applied to our life experiences, brings into view the role of lament in our worship.

A more expansive view of the word *sacred* helps us see that all emotions are valid offerings to God. Just like happiness and joy, sadness and sorrow can be sacred. In fact, lament expressly claims sadness and sorrow as tools of worship and is premised on the idea that we can worship even when praise is not forthcoming. Lament rejects the notion that grief, sorrow, and sadness must be removed before worship can begin. Instead, lament helps us see that grief and sorrow can be given to God—that these emotions can be taken to the altar of the temple—just as readily as happiness and joy can. When we are suffering, we are not without an offering; rather what we have to offer is voiced through the language of lament. And because lament can be given to God, lament is by definition *sacred*. Said differently, lament is the way we worship from *within* our suffering.

Lament is, thus, a critical part of a truly authentic approach to God. Through lament, we are able to validate our experiences of loss, disaster, and tragedy, to claim the grief and sorrow that inevitably accompany such experiences, and then to worship from within our suffering. Lament makes suffering sacred. But this is sometimes not an easy path to walk, and often requires reorienting ourselves. Our proclivity to see pain as less than sacred comes, I think, from a sensibility that tends to view sorrow and grief as something to be avoided and as an indication of some kind of failure or shortcoming on the part of those suffering. Since it seems easier to draw the connection between the "sacred" and the "joyful," it is also easy to wrongly cast sorrow and grief into the pile of "unsacred" things. But when we understand the word "sacred" from the view of the spiritual tradition that Latter-day Saints have inherited from ancient Israel, it becomes clear that "sacredness" has little to do with the inherent nature of things and almost everything to do with how we incorporate these things into our religious practice.

Thus, by recognizing that the feelings of grief, sadness, sorrow, pain, and misery that accompany loss, disaster, and tragedy have the potential to be just as sacred as any other thing given to God, then those who are in the midst of life's storms become free to maintain a relationship with God from within the storm. Granted, the language of lament looks and sounds different than the language of praise, but that fact is simply an acknowledgment of the expansiveness of the human experience and a recognition that our relationship with God is capable of existing through all of it. When we cannot yet say, "My God delivered me," we may still be able to say, "My God, my God, why hast thou forsaken me?" Both are statements of relationship and fidelity; both are sacred; both are worship. It is in this way that lament becomes a lifeline, not because it pulls us out of our problems, but because lament gives us a way to hold onto God even while we suffer.

A SACRED LIFELINE

We have already seen a few examples in which lament has served as a lifeline for individuals who claim grief and sorrow for worship and maintain their relationship with God in the midst of sorrow and grief. For the likes of Jeremiah and Joseph Smith, lament was a way to maintain worship and maintain a relationship in the midst of suffering and pain. On the cross, Jesus used the language of lament to express fidelity from within his feelings of abandonment. In fact, once we can recognize lament for what it is—faithful worship exercised by those endeavoring to hold on—examples abound. For instance, the hymn

"Lead, Kindly Light" (based on the text of the 1834 poem) begins with heart-wrenching language reminiscent of Psalm 31:

Lead, kindly Light, amid the encircling gloom,
 Lead Thou me on!
The night is dark, and I am far from home—
 Lead Thou me on![4]

Another hymn, "Where Can I Turn for Peace?" begins with language of lament reminiscent of Psalm 33:

Where can I turn for peace?
Where is my solace
When other sources cease to make me whole?
When with a wounded heart, anger, or malice,
I draw myself apart,
Searching my soul?[5]

This anonymously composed African American spiritual, which has echoes of Psalm 88, reflects a portion of the misery caused by the slave trade:

Sometimes I feel like a motherless child. . . .
Sometimes I feel like I'm almost gone. . . .
A long ways from home, a long ways from home.[6]

Lament does not avoid the pain or seek to hide from it. Rather—as Dombkowski Hopkins notes when she discusses the grief she felt at the death of her brother—laments are a "lifeline to God and the church in [our] anger and confusion."[7] In these examples, as in other instances (which are so numerous that they cannot be catalogued), lament serves as a lifeline for those in pain. Lament is how those who are tempest-tossed in the ocean of life's journey tie themselves to the deck of the ship of faith. In those moments when the storm threatens to sink our ship, rather than pretending there is no storm or jumping overboard under the assumption that leaving the ship will cause the storm to pass, lament is the honest recognition of the storm that surrounds us and a voicing of the precarious situation in which we find ourselves. It is, in effect, being willing to say out loud: "This is the worst storm I have ever faced; and I don't know if I will survive. My ship is sinking. I don't like this and I am scared. But I'm holding on, waiting for you to act, God. Where are you?" Lament is when we take our anger and confusion to God, and, by so doing, that anger and confusion become sacred. Lament is our lifeline when the storm is more than we think we can bear.

CHAPTER 6

COMMUNAL LAMENT

COMMUNITIES CAN LAMENT

Earlier, I pointed to examples of loss, disaster, and tragedy that felt so big, so personal, or so deep that *individual* voicelessness is a possible outcome. These are situations from which a praise-focused approach to individual worship may be nearly impossible to imagine. I have suggested thus far that the language of lament gives each of us, individually, the ability to protest the potential silence of sorrow and grief and to find language to worship from within loss, disaster, and tragedy. Lament gives each of us, individually, the tools to hold on in the midst of individual challenges; lament is how we hold on to God even while we may feel overwhelmed with individual grief and sorrow.

However, Christianity is also a *communal* practice. As Alma prepared his followers for baptism, the scriptures say that he taught "them" (see Mosiah 18:7) and, when his followers expressed their desire to be baptized, they responded collectively: "This is the desire of *our* hearts" (Mosiah 18:11; emphasis added). This is reminiscent of a story found earlier in the book of Mosiah, when King Benjamin also teaches his people collectively. At the end of his sermon, his people's expression of faith is recorded as being spoken "with one voice" (Mosiah 5:2). Paul said that we, collectively, are "baptized into one body" and make up "the body of Christ" (1 Corinthians 12:13, 27). And Elder D. Todd Christofferson gave an entire general conference address in October 2015 entitled "Why the Church," in which he explored the critical nature of our Church community, noting that a community is required for our individual and collective progress. But worship communities are more than just the Church at large. Worship communities include all of the groups found within the Church (Young Men and Young Women groups, wards, stakes, quorums, Relief Society, Primary and Sunday School classes, etc.). Worship communities also include our families. And close friends—those with whom we choose to share life's journey—can also become worship communities. Even community organizations, especially those that are grounded in strong ethical or religious ideals, can serve as worship communities. In the view of Christ's gospel, a worship community is any place where two or three are gathered in his name (see Matthew 18:20). We cannot be true Christians in isolation. Christianity *requires* community. Christianity is a team sport.

The impacts of this reality are striking. Not only are we to do all we can do individually to live Christian lives, but as a Christian community (or as Christian communit*ies*), we must also collectively act according to our collective commitments. Further, not only are we called to practice authentic individual worship; we are also called to practice authentic communal worship. That is one reason we have church services and ward and stake activities—worshipping together is part of what it means to be Christian. And, therefore (specific to this conversation), just as authentic individual worship includes—and we must all make room for—individual lament, it must also be the case that authentic communal worship should include communal lament. And the importance of communal lament (like the importance of personal lament) is also found in the scriptures.

For instance, Daniel Belnap, a Latter-day Saint scholar, finds that the Psalter's communal laments are expressly connected to covenant-making practices found in the Hebrew Bible and reflect the reality of "a *community* bound to God with a covenant."[1] But, perhaps the clearest example of this is found in Alma's teachings at the Waters of Mormon. Alma taught that among the covenants made at baptism was the commitment to "mourn with those that mourn" (Mosiah 18:9). In the context of Alma's communal teaching and that group's communal acceptance of the covenant, this charge can certainly be read to suggest that a *collective* commitment to acknowledge *collective* mourning is a central part of what it means to be a Christian community. But why? Because, in the same way that individual lament helps individuals maintain relationality with God in the face of individual crises, the practice of communal lament helps communities maintain relationality with God in the face of community crises.

Similar to the way that this might play out in one's personal life, there are also examples of loss, disaster, and tragedy that feel so big and so deep that collective silence is a possible outcome. For those in the United States, the terrorist attacks of September 11, 2001, could be viewed as one such moment; it was hard for our worship communities to know what to say in the immediate aftermath of that tragedy. But such dramatic, identifiable events are not the only times when community silence is a possible outcome. For instance, how can we enjoy a potluck dinner together if we consider that millions are without food and that a child dies from hunger every ten seconds?[2] How are we as a community to worship each Sunday when we know that, at that exact moment, there are atrocities being committed in conflict zones across the world? How can our congregations sing hymns of praise at the opening and closing of our sacrament meetings when we know that as we sing, other humans are being sold into slavery? How can we engage in spiritual conversations during a Sunday School lesson, when sexism, racism, homophobia, and other forms of social violence are making victims of our brothers and sisters? As communities, we may not have the language to grapple with these overwhelming situations and may feel unable to find a collective way to express sadness and grief.

Because of the crippling effect such realizations can have, silence can feel attractive. This kind of collective silence can be manifested in many ways. Sometimes our communities of worship may simply ignore the scale and scope of pain that currently exists, or at least try not to think about it much. Perhaps sometimes our worship communities may seek to explain away such suffering as being "deserved." Or perhaps sometimes our worship communities may dismiss such suffering as unfortunate but ultimately outside of our control. Or perhaps sometimes our worship communities may simply say nothing because such suffering is considered as part of God's plan. The point is that, too often, when faced with the reality of the scale and scope of loss, disaster, and tragedy that is present in the world at large, our worship communities' default is often to retreat into praise-only language in an attempt to bandage our own wounds. And the practical outcome is that we end up ignoring the very suffering we have been called to heal. Said more directly: given the magnitude of suffering all around, a praise-only approach to worship (most especially in wealthy nations and communities) can lead us into willful ignorance of or indifference to suffering. It is an unfortunate fact of history that among the very first things taken from the oppressed is their voice, and among the very first things expunged from the public record is the reality of their suffering.

So, when we as communities become aware of loss, disaster, and tragedy on a community or global scale, the language of lament gives our communities the ability to protest the potential silence of sorrow and grief and to find language that fosters collective worship even as it acknowledges this loss, disaster, and tragedy. As with individual worship, lament gives a way for communities to validate the painful emotions we and others feel when faced with suffering on a community or global scale, and then to claim those feelings of grief and sorrow for worship. It does not require that the grief, sorrow, and sadness of an incident be ignored or that such feelings go away before worship can begin, but rather, communal lament is the vehicle that allows our communities to worship from within their collective suffering.

Lament gives our communities the tools to hold on in the midst of community challenges; a way to hold on to God in the midst of community grief and sorrow.

COMMUNITIES SHOULD LAMENT

I have come to believe that communal lament is just as important as individual lament. I am not alone in this. In the global sense, Brueggemann expresses this idea eloquently. He says, "The recovery of personal lament psalms is a great gain, but unless the communal laments are set alongside, the record of personal religion can serve privatistic concerns—and that is no doubt a betrayal of biblical faith."[3]

And Gustavo Gutierrez, one of the fathers of liberation theology, asserted that the Christian community's task is "to find the words with which to talk about God in the midst of the starvation of millions, the humiliation of races regarded as inferior, discrimination against women, a persistent high rate of infant mortality, those who simply 'disappear' or are deprived of their freedom, the sufferings of peoples who are struggling for their right to live, the exiles and the refugees, terrorism of every kind, and the corpse-filled graves of Ayacucho."[4]

More locally, Bishop Richard C. Edgley points to the many ways in which individual wards across the world "endure together" in the face of pain, suffering, and distress by directly addressing the challenges that surround individuals and communities.[5] All three suggest that, far from being an accoutrement to Christian faith, the ability for our communities to (1) *see* and to (2) *commiserate* with the suffering of others—that is, our ability to practice communal lament—is part and parcel of our Christian commitment.

The views of Brueggemann, Gutierrez, and Edgley are validated by teachings in the Book of Mormon and in the Bible. As was already mentioned, at the Waters of Mormon, Alma taught that the Christian vocation required mourning with those who mourn. Implicit in this covenant commitment is the foundational truth that in order to mourn with those who mourn, our community must first *see* those who are mourning and then be able, as a community, to *commiserate* with their suffering. Latter-day Saint scholar James Faulconer observes that King Benjamin takes this even further and encourages us (as a body of believers) to identify with "the beggar," a collective term that signals a group of people who are in need (Mosiah 4:19).[6] Again, the ability to identify with "the beggar" requires our communities to see and commiserate with their grief and sorrow. In the Bible, the Israelites as a whole are encouraged multiple times to identify with and take care of "the stranger, the widow, the orphan," also collective terms that point to groups of people who may be in need (see, for example, Exodus 22:21; 23:9; Leviticus 19:33; Deuteronomy 10:9).[7] And, again, the ability to identify with these groups requires that communities see and commiserate with others' pain and struggles.

To be clear, this is no easy task. Once we as communities are truly able to see and commiserate with the grief and sorrow of other communities—mourners, beggars, strangers, widows, and orphans—we begin to bear a heavy load. Their collective need becomes our collective need, their collective suffering becomes our collective suffering, their collective pain becomes our collective pain. We begin to bear their sorrows as our own. Carrying such a load may seem to pose a challenge to our faith in whether or not God has concern for the weakest among us. But it need not be thus. As we bear this load, our worship communities can draw on the power of communal lament. As communities, we can worship through lament in the *plural*. "I" becomes "we", "my" becomes "our"; "me" becomes "us." As a group, we join in solidarity with those who hurt; as a worship community, we hold on to each other and to covenant *alongside* those who are suffering. In a very real sense, lament *joins* our communities together. With that in mind, pay attention to the way plural pronouns are used in these examples of communal lament and perhaps consider what it means to lament alongside and with those communities for whom this language resonates.

O God, why hast thou cast us off for ever? . . .
  Have respect unto the covenant:
for the dark places of the earth are full of the habitations of
  cruelty.
  O let not the oppressed return ashamed.
(PSALM 74:1, 20–21)

We are become a reproach to our neighbours,
  a scorn and derision to them that are round about us. . . .
Help us, O God of our salvation.
(PSALM 79:4, 9)

Awake, why sleepest thou, O LORD?
  arise, cast us not off for ever.
Wherefore hidest thou thy face,
  and forgettest our affliction and our oppression?
For our soul is bowed down to the dust:
  our belly cleaveth unto the earth.
Arise for our help, and redeem us for thy mercies' sake.
(PSALM 44:23–26)

As worship communities truly identify with others' suffering, we can, together, authentically lament alongside and with those who are suffering—as our Christian vocation demands. Indeed, when faced with such suffering, our most authentic response is to engage in communal lament.

THE SURPRISING OUTCOMES OF COMMUNAL LAMENT

As is the case with individual lament, the community is stronger when it incorporates communal lament into its spiritual arsenal. Though there are likely many different ways in which this occurs, I will focus on three specific ways in which this plays out.

First, when used as an intentional spiritual practice, the practice of communal lament serves to reinforce within our communities the interconnectedness of our small worship communities with all humanity. Because authentic communal lament is premised on the ability to see and commiserate with those groups who suffer, worship communities that are open to communal lament are more clearly able to recognize that their destiny is tied up with our destiny (to paraphrase Martin Luther King Jr.).[8] Brueggemann expressed the same idea when he noted that communal lament "permits us to remember that we are indeed public citizens and creatures and have an immediate, direct, and personal stake in public events . . . [and helps] overcome our general religious abdication of public issues and the malaise of indifference and apathy that comes with abdication."[9] Former First Counselor in the Relief Society General Presidency Chieko Okazaki reminds us simply, "We are all connected."[10] The fact is that as we more regularly introduce and make room for communal lament, our worship communities can more easily recognize that we, the community, suffer when starvation exists anywhere; we, the community, are damaged by discrimination of any kind; we, the community, are victimized when violence persists; we, the community, are made weaker when the humanity of those who are "others" is rejected. As worship communities truly identify with others' suffering and authentically lament alongside and with those who are suffering, our communities expressly connect the cause of all humankind (and creation itself—recall that in Moses 7:48, the earth itself laments) and protest against the silence that accompanies loss, disaster, and tragedy. In so doing, we answer the call to become of one heart and one mind (see Moses 7:18; 4 Nephi 1:1–2).

Second, practicing communal lament opens our eyes to the reality that others may need the space to lament even if we do not. When the lament is not a central part of our individual worship practices, it is easy to neglect those around us who may be in dire need of such language. And, thus, if lament were preserved only for individual worship, we each might forget about the power of lament when we are, individually, able to use the language of praise. By making space for communal lament, even while we may individually reside in a place where praise comes easily, we are each reminded of the need to consider that others, in their suffering, may need to be able to voice lament. We might ask ourselves, as Brueggemann does, "Who needs to pray that way [via lament] today?"[11] Communal lament forces us, in the best way possible, to remember that, at any point in time, those around us may be suffering under the weight of grief and sorrow. The act of communal lament is, thus, an act of solidarity and a way to ensure that our communities continually make space for those whose worship can *only* be expressed with lament.

Third, and perhaps most importantly, the act of communal lament is a rejection of the status quo and a form of faithful resistance against the structures that allow such suffering to occur in the first place. Commenting on theologian Dorothee Soelle's insight that "the first step toward overcoming suffering is, then, to find language that leads out of the uncomprehended suffering that makes one mute," Dombkowski Hopkins observes, "Communication by lament brings solidarity in which change and liberation can occur."[12] As Arthur Green puts it, in our crying out via lament we acknowledge that "we have seen the arbitrariness of fate, the depths of human cruelty, the indifference of both man and nature. . . . We stare into the face of darkness and proclaim that light still exists. We refuse to give in to hopelessness. The struggle for faith and the refusal to give in are one and the same."[13]

Said simply, communal lament is a community's way of asking, "How could this happen?" and then asserting, "This is terrible and should not have happened; we cannot let it happen ever again." Thus, as one commentator notes, "Lament is not simply feeling bad. . . . Lament is not simply feeling sad . . . [or] passive acceptance of a tragedy . . . [or] weakly assenting to the status quo . . . [or] the expression of sorrow in order to assuage feelings of guilt and the burden of responsibility;" rather, "lament responds."[14] Communal lament is a form of faithful resistance against the powers of oppression. In our acts of communal lament, we are collectively clinging to that God in whom we trust and refusing to allow the cruelty that surrounds us to persist unnoticed and unchecked. Far from being an admission of weakness, communal lament for communal suffering—including the suffering for which our earthly institutions bear responsibility—is a demonstration of our community's faith in God, shows the strength of our commitment to communal covenant keeping, and is a sign of our community's willingness to move toward wholeness together. President M. Russell Ballard suggested, "Perhaps there has never been a more important time for neighbors all around the world to stand together for the common good of one another."[15]

A BRIEF DIVERSION ON WHAT LAMENT MIGHT LOOK LIKE

Thus far, I have tried to make the case that lament is a critical component of our individual and communal worship lives. I have done so without offering any suggestions for application or personal examples, and that was by design. So, before I offer some ideas for what lament might look like "in real life" to embrace individual and communal lament more fully, let me explain a little bit about why I have waited so long to offer these ideas.

First, I did this because I wanted to unquestioningly ground the spiritual practice of lament *within* the Latter-day Saint faith tradition. It is my experience that for members of The Church of Jesus Christ of Latter-day Saints, and for Christians more generally, learning to see lament as part of and necessary for a truly authentic covenant relationship with God can require unlearning cultural scripts and tendencies. It requires adopting a theological vocabulary that seems foreign at first and embracing new worship patterns that might be initially uncomfortable. This kind of reorientation can be challenging, especially when a praise-only approach is still so prominent in modern Christian culture. Thus, I wanted to avoid any sense of "I like this, so you might too"—as if lament is an optional gospel accessory that we can put on or take off as a matter of preference. Rather, I hoped to drive home the reality that a covenant relationship without lament is ultimately incomplete, and it is not just me saying that—this truth is reinforced as far back as ancient scripture goes. Said differently, by intentionally "depersonalizing" this discussion and instead focusing on the scriptural and spiritual foundations of lament, I hope to establish beyond any doubt that lament is an essential aspect of faith in the God of Abraham, Isaac, and Jacob. Lament *is* part of a life of faith. Full stop.

Second, though I recognize the value that ideas for application or personal examples might offer for some, I feel a great sense of trepidation that any suggestions or examples I offer will be taken as normative descriptions of how lament should work in others' lives. Because lament is connected to those moments when we might be the most unsettled—those moments in life when loss and tragedy loom over everything—lament is, of necessity, a situationally driven spiritual practice. So, what works for one person or community in a given situation may not work for another person or community in another situation. In fact, each of us will need to apply lament in whatever way makes the most sense for each of our individual lives and within our communities. Showing what lament might look like in one person's life could unintentionally lead someone else to believe that he or she is "doing lament wrong" or that there is a "right way" to lament. So even as I offer some examples here, it is always true that the way lament works for me may not work for others. I want to avoid any sense that the examples I offer should constrain anyone else in how lament plays out in their own lives.

Third, I have avoided the application of these ideas and personal examples of lament because I was concerned that I might imply that only certain sources of sorrow, grief, and pain are appropriate sources for lament and other sources of sorrow, grief, and pain are not. Already, I fear I have unintentionally suggested that lament is only appropriate for "big" moments of sorrow, grief, and pain. It is easy to point to enormous tragedies when discussing the role of lament in worship; rhetorically, stark examples make for clear descriptions. But the reality is that the situations in life that result in the kind of sorrow, grief, and pain from which lament springs are as varied as the

A BRIEF DIVERSION ON WHAT LAMENT MIGHT LOOK LIKE

individual him/herself. For some, the death of a grandparent might not be terribly traumatic, and for others this event could be deeply painful; for some, not getting invited to a friend's gathering might not matter in the slightest, and for others it could be soul-crushing. There is no sign that says, "Your tragedy must be at least this big in order to require lament" (to paraphrase Elder Dieter F. Uchtdorf's famous line about testimony).[1] In providing some examples of lament, I hope no one feels that lament is something that is okay for "other people and their experiences but not for me and my experiences."

Finally, my lived experience is limited. I have certainly experienced sorrow, grief, and pain in my life. But I have never faced the death of a spouse or child, I have never become homeless due to job loss, I have never been the victim of violent crime, I have never been caught in a civil war, I have never not had enough food to eat, and I have never been diagnosed with a terminal illness, as just a few examples. Because I have never had these experiences (and many, many others), I am simply not in a position to suggest how lament looks for individuals who *have had* those experiences. And, thus, I worry that in providing personal examples I might fail to capture an important nuance in how lament might work for those whose sorrow, grief, and pain are different than mine. Consistent with some of the points made earlier, the beauty of lament is that it is fundamentally about authentic, covenant connection. And that covenant connection occurs person by person, situation by situation, and moment by moment. I pray that any personal examples I offer will not get in the way of understanding that.

Having now laid out the reasons I have waited so long, I do recognize that ideas for application and personal examples can be valuable. Just because I have not had every experience with lament does not mean I have no experience with lament. So, I am going to approach this in two ways. To begin with, I will offer a variety of general suggestions for how a fuller embrace of lament might play out in our lives and communities. These suggestions could be organized in a few different ways, but I am going to look at it from the lens of concentric and ever-widening circles: the personal, the familial, the church community, and the local, national, and worldwide community. To be clear, these ideas are just a starting point for reflection; they are not a complete list nor a perfectly well-framed list. Perhaps some of what is suggested will work for you and your communities, and perhaps some ideas will not. That is fine. The point of these suggestions is simply to get the gears in your head and heart turning.

Then, I will provide a few examples of the ways in which I have utilized lament in my own life. Again, to be clear, the personal examples I share are only examples of how lament looked for me in a few specific moments in time as I struggled with things that in those moments were a source of sorrow, grief, and pain.

SUGGESTIONS FOR PERSONAL APPLICATION

Experimenting with personal lament may feel like speaking a foreign language. Especially for those who, like me, were raised within a praise-focused worldview. Having the courage to speak with the candor that we see in Lamentations is potentially frightening. We may not really know how to start. Here are a few specific ideas for opening this door. Where one goes from here is really up to each person:

- *Read and study Lamentations and the lament psalms.* The laments found in Lamentations are easy to identify because the collection comprises its own biblical book. However, lists of lament psalms in the Bible are readily available on the internet or in some of the books I have referenced through the course of this discussion. I have also included a brief list in chapter 2. Simply reading and studying these works can help acclimatize us to the language of lament. You may want to widen your exploration of laments to other places in the standard works. As you read and study these examples, always keep in the front of your mind that this is sacred text and the sentiments expressed in these scriptures are part of the life of worship.

- *Speak scriptural laments out loud.* One of the things for which the King James Version of the Bible is rightly praised is the marvelously poetic language of the text. When you are ready, or have need, read laments aloud. Make them your words. With only a little practice, the poetry of the language will become evident. And, just as you have been taught to claim other teachings in the scriptures as personally applicable (see 1 Nephi 19:23), claim the poetic language of laments in the scriptures as your own. They are part of your heritage too.
- *Pray laments.* It is likely that for most of us, our first steps into lament will come through personal prayer. In the quiet space of prayer, we may have the greatest ability to say those things that are most deeply felt. This is always a good option.
- *Create other forms of lament.* Prayer is not the only option when it comes to lament. It could be that you feel more comfortable writing laments down as prose or poetry (perhaps using the lament outline in chapter 2 as a guide), or speaking them while on a walk or in the car, or going to the top of a mountain or other personal space and shouting until your throat is raw.[2] Or do all of them. The point here is that lament is, foundationally, *worship.* You should do that in whatever way feels the most natural and is likely to foster the most authentic connection with God. Taking complaints to God is among our most sacred actions. It marks our moments of greatest vulnerability and thus creates opportunities for our greatest openness. So do whatever is needed to worship God with this kind of openness and honesty.

SUGGESTIONS FOR FAMILIAL APPLICATION

Most of us have not been taught to "hear" the language of worship in lament. Having read this far, you may now be better equipped than you once were to do that, but that does not mean your family is. So, bring those you call family (whether biologically, as a matter of marriage or other legal connection, or those friends whom you have selected to be your closest allies) into the conversation about lament. It may be easier to go on the journey of lament if you have someone going with you. Again, here are a couple of ideas for practical application:

- *Do the things listed earlier with your family.* Whether it is reading and studying the laments, praying, or creating your own laments, doing these things with other people can help make you more courageous. Journeying into this new space with loved ones has the power to strengthen the bonds of affection as you all authentically acknowledge the need for and the power of lament.
- *Discuss the role of lament in our individual and family life.* Closely connected to the point above is the notion of actually talking about lament. Even if these types of conversations are happening in general church settings (which has not been my experience, but perhaps others have experienced it), the family is still the best place to collectively explore this genre of worship.
- *Make room for lament.* Those you love will eventually need lament. We will all need lament at some point in our lives. Providing this resource to those you love gives them another tool for holding on when times of trial come. Further, lamenting together as a family allows us all to be vulnerable and open with loved ones, which can serve to strengthen our relationships.

SUGGESTIONS FOR CHURCH COMMUNITY APPLICATION

Like much of Christianity, the Latter-day Saint community is fairly praise-focused. Given the messages of hope and restoration Latter-day Saints carry, this is not surprising. However, sometimes our focus on praise elides the importance of using lament to worship. Since the Latter-day Saint community is the one I know best, I am going to limit my observations to this particular church community, but perhaps some of these ideas are more broadly applicable to other denominations:

- *Use lament language in church.* It is my experience that the vast majority of worship exercises are not taught explicitly; rather they are learned mimetically. We see and hear someone do a thing, and then we start to do and say that same thing (think of how quickly a particularly catchy phrase is adopted by the general membership after being used by a prominent leader in general conference). So, when the time is right, use the language of lament at church. This could be in a testimony, talk, or lesson. Whatever the context, faithfully modeling how lament works in your own spiritual life could give others the courage to embrace it too. Further, using this language more often will start to normalize the language of lament. The language of lament may remain evocative and provocative, but the fact that lament is expressed will be less disquieting if we do it more often.
- *Teach the laments.* Because the language of lament can feel scandalous, and because our fellow Latter-day Saints are largely ill-equipped to understand how laments play a role in worship, the lament language in scriptures is often skipped over in our lessons. When you have the chance, highlight the value of lament. When discussing 2 Nephi 4, do not just skip to the "praise language." Instead, reflect on Nephi's expressions of lament and what they

teach you about his faith journey. When discussing D&C 121, spend as much time focused on Joseph's lament as you do on God's answer. When studying the Old Testament, teach the book of Lamentations and do not skip over the lament psalms. We will never get better at embracing the lament tradition if we are not taught how to understand and use it (see Romans 10:14).

- *Let those in our church community lament.* When someone finally does have the courage to speak words of lament out loud, let that lament stand without giving in to the desire to caveat that lament with strategically deployed praise-language. Just mourn with the person who is mourning. Sit with them in their pain and anguish. Let lament have its place. The turn will come, eventually. But let the turn come when it comes; do not try to force it upon them. Above all: never silence lament.

SUGGESTIONS FOR LOCAL, NATIONAL, AND WORLDWIDE COMMUNITY APPLICATION

Many of the items that will be outlined below could have reasonably been put in any (and every) other list above. But these items are put here in order to explore the unique way in which communal lament impacts how we engage in society at large. However, none of the ideas are unique to non-family or non-church communities, and with only a little imagination each of them could be modified to apply in various personal and interpersonal settings.

- *Hear the cries of lament from all around.* In all of our communities, there are groups of people who are getting a raw deal. It is likely that these groups are agitating for change, and we (especially those of us who are somewhat comfortable) might want the "complaining voices" to stop being so loud, direct, or accusatory. But once we recognize that their lament is our lament, and that our wholeness is wrapped up in their wholeness, we can see the importance of hearing their cries—especially when it makes us a little uncomfortable. So, listen to those who are lamenting, and listen most closely to those who do not look like you, sound like you, act like you, or believe like you. It is easy to listen to the lament of those whose voices we recognize; learning to hear the lament of those who are "other" is the essence of Christianity (see Luke 6:32; Matthew 5:46; 1 John 4:20).

- *See and identify with those who are suffering.* Those who suffer are usually on the margins. They are the invisible people who we brush by on the street and who blend into the surroundings. Theirs are the stories that are *not* on the front page of the newspapers and that do *not* pop up on our newsfeed. They are those for whom help is not immediately forthcoming; there is no "return on investment" for helping the landless, poor, and devalued, and thus they are swept aside. Being willing to *see* the suffering of others is a core component of communal lament. Once we learn to see and identify with those who are suffering around us, and once we can lament with and alongside them, we have taken the first step to laying the foundations for newness.

- *Make room for lament.* Some of us—indeed, many of us—reside in a place of relative privilege. From that place of privilege, we have the opportunity to make room for those whose cries we hear and whose suffering we see but who are too far on the margins to be recognized by the power structures that created the inequity in the first place. Too often, the privileged are tempted—once they finally see and hear suffering—to appropriate the lament of those who are suffering and claim it as their own suffering. But such an appropriation is simply another form of silencing; it is just another way of taking away the voice of those who are already marginalized. So, rather than trying to make their argument for them, we can step back and cede our "spot at the table" to those who

suffer and whose laments need to be heard, and then let them express their lament on their own terms. Relinquishing our social power in this way can be hard, but communal lament helps us see that the failure to do so is implicitly valuing status over humanity and comfort over justice.
- *Act.* Recall that lament is rightly seen as an act of protest against both silence and the status quo. And, as will be shown in the next chapter, lament anticipates deliverance and the possibility of newness. So, the spirit of communal lament calls for us to work against the forces that cause that suffering, no matter where they are found. Lament is a response, and that response should include a willingness to act.

LAMENT IN MY LIFE

The general suggestions above, as I hope I have made clear, are not exhaustive. The examples I will soon share from my own life are similarly limited. They reflect only the way one person has used lament in a specific moment to maintain connection with God. Further, in some instances, I did not know what I was doing could be categorized as "lament." But looking back, it was clear that—even if unintentionally—I was using lament as a way to hold on. My sense is that this is true of many people's experiences. Even if one did not realize she or he was utilizing the spiritual practice of lament, upon reflection it is clear that lament was present. My hope is that, going forward, we all can use lament more intentionally and with more self-awareness. If "accidental lament" can be transformational, imagine the power that can come into our lives when lament is intentionally integrated into our worship.

I have made no attempt to categorize or organize these experiences; I will simply let them stand on their own.

9/11: I was a young adult when terrorists crashed commercial

A BRIEF DIVERSION ON WHAT LAMENT MIGHT LOOK LIKE

airplanes into the World Trade Center towers and the Pentagon and into a field in Pennsylvania. I was nearing the end of my undergraduate education and was married and had a young child. As I watched events unfold in real time on the television, I felt my world crumble. So much death. So much destruction. So much uncertainty. So much pain. More than once, I asked myself, my wife, and my God, "Why did this happen? Everything I had thought life would be is now changed! How can I carry on?" In the days that followed, I tried to figure out what it meant to go forward into a world that now included 9/11. I tried to continue to go to classes, but many were canceled, and those that occurred often strayed away from planned material. One particular moment stays with me still: A highly respected professor stood in the front of the classroom on September 12 and wept as he explained that nothing he was planning on talking about mattered much given the events that had just occurred. He encouraged us to go home and be with our families. We all left.

A few days after 9/11, I went to an outdoor gathering spot on campus for a student-organized 9/11 vigil. There, a few hundred students lit candles and milled around in silence. As the sun set, a trumpet player from the university band released the mournful notes of Taps into the stillness. We all sat together in our grief. Though many thoughtful explanations circulated, I could not find a "because" to explain 9/11 (really, there is no way to explain acts like this). I regularly asked God, often with great urgency, why things like 9/11 happen; after all, 9/11 was just one terrible incident among many in human history. In my questioning, I realize now that I was also clinging to God from within my sorrow. I was lamenting.

Over time, my lament turned to action. After long discussions with my wife, I altered my educational plan and I changed my professional path. My grief drove me to embrace a vocation that I had never previously considered. And in this new path I was led into a newness that I could not have imagined. The newness in which I now live embraces the sorrow, grief, and pain that still exist—I will never be able to forget that tragic day—and it builds *out from* that sorrow, grief, and pain. In my protest against despair, and as part of the hope that comes from clinging to a covenant with God, I have tried to make the world a better place for my children.

A family home evening discussion: A few years ago, I attended an event hosted at the Washington D.C. Temple Visitors' Center entitled "The Legacy of Black LDS Pioneers."[3] Throughout the sessions I attended (as a white male whose Church experience did not include many of the stories I heard), I was overwhelmed by the legacy of faithfulness demonstrated by these Church members who, throughout history, overcame hardship after hardship because of their unrelenting and unyielding belief in the restored gospel. I deeply mourned the reality that some of that suffering was the result of now-discarded practices and teachings about race that were common in the past and promulgated by some in Church leadership. And I was pained by the racial inequity that continues to exist in our society. The topic felt urgent, so my wife and I decided to discuss these matters as part of our family home evening. As the discussion moved forward, I found myself without the language to adequately express the deep sorrow I felt. So, I turned to the scriptures. With my voice cracking I read the first verse of Psalm 13 but replaced "me" with "them" (referring to my Black brothers and sisters), "How long wilt thou forget [them], O Lord? for ever? how long wilt thou hide thy face from [them]?" As the verse ended, I broke down in tears.

What followed was a quiet moment of sacredness that I shared with my wife and young children. I cannot explain it any better than that. God was present, and even without answers, presence was enough. I do not know for certain if that moment impacted my family the way it impacted me, but as I voiced that lament I felt a connection with God that was palpable, and I resolved in that moment that for the rest of my life I would do my part to fight inequity in all its forms.

A BRIEF DIVERSION ON WHAT LAMENT MIGHT LOOK LIKE

I continue to try to keep that commitment in any way that is within my power. I want to be one of the tools that God uses to bring about the world in which we are all "fellow citizens" (See Ephesians 2:19; Galatians 3:28).

Sunday School: As I prepared to guide a Sunday School discussion that included Doctrine and Covenants 121 as part of the material for the week, I felt deeply moved by Joseph Smith's lament. It was my distinct impression that the class should spend most of the time focused on this and other examples of lament. In that discussion we read the opening verses of section 121 and parts of 2 Nephi chapter 4, and we read Jesus's use of lament psalms on the cross, and then some of the lament psalms themselves. As a small part of Christ's body, we discussed the role of lament in our lives and the deep faithfulness that lament demonstrates. Any desire to find a "because" was replaced by a fierce fidelity to God from within sorrow, grief, and pain. Some members of the class were visibly moved and shared hallowed moments when they used lament to cling onto a covenant relationship. For my part, more than once I had to make an extra effort to maintain my composure as I listened to the words of faithful sorrow expressed by those in that class.

As the fifty-minute discussion ended, it seemed to me we were closer as a group. We did not leave that day with answers. But in openly sharing our laments, we deepened our covenant relationships with God and with each other.

The Holocaust Museum: In our school system, students read *Anne Frank: The Diary of a Young Girl* as part of their middle school experience, usually connected with a unit about World War II. It has been our family's practice, around the time when each of our children have these discussions at school, to take that child to the United States Holocaust Memorial Museum in Washington, D.C. It is never easy, but it is always important. As my children each make their way through the museum and grapple with the reality of what happened in the Holocaust, each has asked, in his or her own way, questions like, "How can people do this to each other?" and "Why didn't God stop this from happening?" I am never able to answer those questions. I usually respond with something along the lines of, "Honestly, I don't know; but it must never happen again."

The journey through the museum ends in the Hall of Remembrance. It is a simple, uncluttered space in the shape of a hexagon. The focal point is a flame that never goes out, and on the walls are inscribed the names of concentration and death camps; light filters in through small windows on the ceiling and the walls. It is a space of reflection that I find to be profoundly holy. In that room, we have allowed ourselves to feel sorrow, grief, and pain (in the small way that we can) for the atrocities of the Holocaust, and we have asked the hard questions about why God allows such things to occur. I have wept in that room more than once. Without answers, we cling to covenant through lament.

Faith: I have always been drawn to belief in God—from my youngest years I have had a sense of and felt a connection to the Divine. The Latter-day Saint community gave me a powerful vocabulary to express my belief and offered an expansive and exciting theology. As part of my participation in the Latter-day Saint community, I had numerous experiences in which I felt divine presence, I grew in my understanding of truth and light, and I embraced my relationship with God through covenant making. And yet, even with all of these experiences under my belt, some years ago my faith began to deconstruct. I will not discuss the specific details of the challenges I faced, but in the end I felt nearly hopeless and faithless, and deeply uncertain about what to do next. I have described this as entering "the wilderness" or as watching a house explode, with nothing but scattered remnants remaining. I felt forsaken, unmoored, and disoriented.

For me, this was a time of sorrow, grief, and pain. But I made a choice to hold on to a relationship with God even as everything else fell apart. I watched the faith of my youth and young adulthood die. I mourned the loss of that faith and grieved for its passing. I took that mourning and grief to God; I offered God my pain because it was all I had left to give.

Slowly, I discovered that "the wilderness" was, inextricably, a place of divine care and nourishment. A landscape that had looked barren and desolate in the beginning was, in fact, a place of new life; it was where God nurtured me and guided me. Because "the wilderness" was a place where I *had to* rely on God, it ended up being the place where *I found* God. And gradually, as I inspected the scattered remnants of my old faith, I realized that the "house of faith" from my youth and young adulthood had not been properly constructed in the first place. As I closely examined the materials that made up my "house of faith" I came to see that, though much of the core material was still good, my house needed to be put back together in a different way. So, I began, piece by piece, the process of reconstruction. It was a reconstruction that could not have occurred without a complete razing of the old structure.

Now, years later, "the wilderness" seems further away—but I do not fear wildernesses anymore. And many days, it feels like my house of faith is more firmly grounded than ever—but I do not fear reconstruction. As painful as the journey into the wilderness and the process of reconstruction were, I experienced a kind of deliverance that was totally unexpected. And through all the sorrow and grief that I felt, I have found a newness that is beyond anything I could have imagined. I remember the sorrow, grief, and pain of the past; those feelings are not gone. Quite the contrary, those emotions are now *part* of my journey of faith. They are part of what binds me to God.

INTERLUDE

THEODICY

In the next chapter of this book, which is the final chapter, I will explore the hope for newness and anticipation of deliverance that is baked into lament. However, before going forward, I feel it is important to briefly discuss theodicy, which has been a backdrop through this entire exploration of lament.

Theodicy is a theological term that comes from the Greek *theos* ("God") and *dikē* ("justice/judgment"). In its most basic form, it poses the question, "How do we explain the fact that a good God allows/permits bad things to happen?"[1] Brueggemann offered this pithy definition: "Theodicy is concern for a *fair deal*."[2] Why does God allow cancer to grow in some people (or why does God give cancer to some people) but not others? Why does God allow some people to be born into (or why does God put some people into) abject poverty and others into wealth and luxury? Why are some people allowed to become (or why does God make some people) victims of sex trafficking while others live in empowering, nurturing environments? How can we reconcile faith in a just God when the world is filled with obvious cases of the powerful exploiting the weak? Elder Dale G. Renlund described this as "infuriating unfairness,"[3] and Elder Quentin L. Cook notes that questions like this are "among the most frequently asked questions of Church leaders."[4] These questions, and a million more like them, are crushingly challenging questions. Though responses like, "Everything happens for a reason and God is in charge!" are often tossed out quickly, for many (and I include myself in this group), these statements feel less like a statement of faith and more like (1) a willful ignorance that can be maintained only from a position of privilege, (2) a bald-faced refusal to acknowledge the reality and scale of the injustice that exists, and/or (3) an unwillingness to seriously consider the questions theodicy poses. My sense is that theodicy is a matter with which all those who profess a covenant relationship with God must eventually grapple.[5]

As I hope is clear by now, the spiritual practice of lament makes no attempt to resolve questions surrounding theodicy; that is to say, lament does not seek to explain (or explain away) loss, disaster, and tragedy. Quite the contrary; lament simply validates that those things happen and then claims the resulting sorrow and grief as a foundation for worship. Lament does not feel required to jump to God's defense (in other words, it does not try to intuit why challenges arrive); rather, lament takes as a foundational principle that God is willing to hear our cries of pain and anguish. Lament asks God "why?" and "how?" but does not offer a "because." It is in this way that lament is a valuable spiritual practice.

Lament is one way in which individuals and worship communities try to deal with the contradictions and challenges that theodicy poses. As Brueggemann explains, the myriad examples of laments in sacred texts make clear that "Israel is not interested in spirituality or communion with God that tries to deny or obscure the important issues of theodicy. An unjust relation with God is no relation at all. A skewed communion is not a communion worth having."[6] In fact, a primary attribute of lament language is the boldness to ask God directly, "How can you, God, allow this to happen?" Thus, as Amy-Jill Levine and Marc Brettler note, because "many of the psalmists of lament are convinced of their own innocence," these statements of lament "can be understood as protest literature that addresses the problem of theodicy."[7] As a case in point, consider the example of Job, who, according to the text was "perfect and upright" (Job 1:1) and yet suffered terribly. From the midst of his suffering, and consistent with what we have already discussed about lament, Job asks boldly: "Why do the wicked live on, reach old age, and grow mighty in power?" (Job 21:7, NRSV). Job's faithful lament is, at its core, a protest against his situation, which is itself premised on the problem of theodicy.

Importantly, even though God speaks with Job, Job's question is really never addressed. It is true that, at the end of his story, Job is restored to health, gets a new family, and comes into new riches. But none of these things resolve his question about whether or not his suffering—his loss of health, the death of his first family, and his destitution—was just.[8] Further, the physical, mental, and spiritual scars that accompanied Job's loss likely remained with him to the end of his days regardless of the largess that came when his suffering ended. For Job, and for all of us, the challenge of theodicy remains. The point I hope to drive home on theodicy is this: As long as there has been a belief in God, believers have grappled with theodicy. If there were an easy answer to this question, it would be readily available. But such answers are not easy, and seemingly easy answers are often not answers at all. However, in the face of this apparent injustice, one way to faithfully respond is lament. We may not ever understand the "because" of suffering, but lament teaches us that faith in God and belief in the covenant does not mean we need to accept injustice. That is to say, when faced with the challenge of theodicy, lament is the tool given to us to faithfully say to God, "I do not think this is fair!"

Loss, disaster, and tragedy strike all of us. It happens to those in our immediate communities and to those on the other side of the world. Individually, the ability to lament can be one way we hold on to a covenant relationship. Similarly, as we come to see and identify with the suffering and injustice that exists in the world—as is demanded by our Christian vocation—lament is a tool of covenantal relationship for our communities. In fact, when we really ponder the vastness and intensity of the suffering that exists all around, it is hard to imagine how anyone can retain a true, honest covenant relationship with Deity without the ability to lament.

CHAPTER 7

FINDING NEWNESS (EVENTUALLY)

NEW POSSIBILITIES

So far, we have discussed the reality that happiness and sadness are not only part of life, but central components of life's journeys. We need each to understand and appreciate the other. Rather than making us less like our heavenly parents, the ability to discern the bitter from the sweet moves us forward in our eternal progression. But how, then, are we to maintain a relationship with God while we are in the midst of earthly sorrows? One clear answer is the spiritual practice of lament. Lament is a particular kind of language that can be used for engaging God in moments of distress. I have suggested that this genre provides individuals and communities a powerful—really irreplaceable—tool for maintaining our covenant connection to God in the midst of loss, disaster, and tragedy. Lament does this by claiming the sorrow and grief that inevitably arise when such moments arrive and then using them as the foundation for worship. Our pain becomes sacred as we offer it—authentically, openly, and without reservation—to God.

But what comes *after* lament? Sprinkled throughout the discussion thus far—and especially in the story of Hannah and some of the examples I just shared—have been allusions to the reality that lament does not go on perpetually. Eventually, the old thing passes away, and newness takes its place. That is what we explore in this chapter. Of necessity, this chapter will move into ideas that are more ephemeral because we are moving from the certainty of what *is* to the possibilities of what *could be*. Thus, we will circle around the concept of newness and view it from different angles. The radical openness of God's newness invites, perhaps even demands, this kind of opacity. We simply cannot predict how newness will manifest in our lives and in the world. That is part of the wonder of newness—it is new. With that caveat, this last chapter will look at the sometimes slow process that allows lament to turn into praise. Be warned: those looking for easy answers or surefire formulas will, unfortunately, be disappointed. Though the reality of deliverance is almost always on the horizon of lament, the timing of that deliverance is not ours to decide, and the nature of that deliverance is—in almost all instances—well beyond our mortal vision and outside our imagination. Time and patience are required. But newness, a marvelous newness, will come.

DELIVERANCE AND LIBERATION

Psalm 32 contains a surprising admission of guilt alongside an intense expression of faith. As with other lament psalms, the psalmist notes the grief and sorrow that is felt: "My bones waxed old through my roaring all the day long. For day and night thy [the Lord's] hand was heavy upon me: my moisture is turned into the drought of summer" (Psalm 32:3–4). Yet, unlike some lament psalms, in Psalm 32, the psalmist admits personal sin is a likely cause of grief. Says the psalmist: "I acknowledged my sin unto thee, and mine iniquity have I not hid. I said, I will confess my transgressions unto the Lord" (Psalm 32:5). What is most remarkable, however, is that as the psalmist expresses the cry of lament and admits to wrongdoing, the psalmist also asserts powerfully: "Thou art my hiding place; thou shalt preserve me from trouble; thou shalt compass me about with songs of deliverance" (Psalm 32:7). How is it that the God whose "hand was heavy upon me" because of "mine iniquity" is also "my hiding place" who will "preserve me from trouble" and "compass me about with songs of deliverance"? How can the psalmist express all three of those ideas in the same breath? What is the source of such honesty with and faith in God?

The answer is that lament is premised on belief in a God that delivers and liberates. Ancient Israel's earliest history includes experiences of deliverance and liberation from the most extreme of circumstances. Recall that during a time of famine in Canaan, the family of Israel (Jacob) left Canaan and settled in Egypt. Initially, because of the well-connected Joseph, Israel and his family were welcomed by the Pharaoh and given the land of Goshen (see Genesis 47:1–11). However, as generations rolled on and the Israelite family grew, the Israelites became perceived by the Egyptian leadership as a threat (see Exodus 1:7–8).[1] To neutralize the threat, the Israelites were put to work as slaves making bricks for Pharaoh (see Exodus 1:11–14; 5:4–14). The Israelites, a once-cared-for group of refugees, were now a landless group of foreigners (strangers, exiles, migrants—these words often work as synonyms in the scriptures) enslaved by the most powerful force on earth. This was a disastrous change of circumstance. And the Israelites reacted in exactly the way one might expect. They "cried out." The scriptures do not give us the language of this cry, but it seems reasonable to me that their expressions of lament might have been something like: *Why are we enslaved? We do not remember freedom. How can this be? Our burden is heavier than we can bear.* And the result of this lament? God heard them and responded with deliverance and liberation. Here is how the story is recounted in the scriptures:

> The Israelites groaned under their slavery, and cried out. Out of the slavery their cry for help rose up to God. God heard their groaning, and God remembered his covenant with Abraham, Isaac, and Jacob. God looked upon the Israelites, and God took notice of them. . . . Then the Lord said, "I have observed the misery of my people who

are in Egypt; I have heard their cry on account of their taskmasters. Indeed, I know their sufferings, and I have come down to deliver them from the Egyptians, and to bring them up out of that land to a good and broad land, a land flowing with milk and honey." (Exodus 2:23–25; 3:7–8, NRSV)

We see a similar pattern after the Israelites leave Egypt and find themselves in the vastness of the wilderness. Recall that the departure from Egypt was rapid (Exodus 12:33) and the ability to gather supplies was limited (they did not even have time to wait for leavened bread, hence the use of unleavened bread at Passover celebrations). While in the wilderness, the Israelites—perhaps not surprisingly—wondered if starving in the wilderness was any better than dying as slaves to Pharaoh. The Israelites lamented their situation (in a way that feels a little petty, if we are being honest). But, again, God heard them, and God delivered them. Here is how this story is recorded:

> [In the wilderness] the Israelites said to [Moses and Aaron], "If only we had died by the hand of the LORD in the land of Egypt, when we sat by the fleshpots and ate our fill of bread; for you have brought us out into this wilderness to kill this whole assembly with hunger." . . . The LORD spoke to Moses and said, "I have heard the complaining of the Israelites; say to them, 'At twilight you shall eat meat, and in the morning you shall have your fill of bread; then you shall know that I am the LORD your God.'" In the evening quails came up and covered the camp; and in the morning there was a layer of dew around the camp. When the layer of dew lifted, there on the surface of the wilderness was a fine flaky substance, as fine as frost on the ground. (Exodus 16:3, 11–14, NRSV)

These very early stories of deliverance became a paradigmatic frame of reference that was used over and over again by later prophets and was a key piece of how Israel understood its covenant relationship with God. One scholar explains it this way: "The prophets (for example, Jeremiah, Ezekiel, and Hosea) frequently cite the divine redemption of the exodus to rebuke Israel for being faithless and ungrateful but also to encourage Israel during the exile with a promise of deliverance even greater than the exodus (Isa 43). . . . In the Psalms (particularly Ps 29:3–4, Ps 29:10, and Ps 78), the exodus also reminds Israel of divine rescue, often in terms of the cosmos and nature as well as history."[2] Even more powerfully, perhaps, the scriptures say that these events of deliverance are also how God sees the relationship with Israel and the way in which *God* chooses to express the nature of the covenantal relationship between God and Israel. The act of deliverance out of Egypt and into Canaan is cited by God repeatedly as proof of *God's faithfulness to Israel* (see, for example, Exodus 19:4; 20:2; Leviticus 26:1–2, 13; Deuteronomy 5:6; 15:15; and Psalm 81:10). That is to say, God understands and shows covenantal commitment to Israel via acts of deliverance. Though this is not the only theological tradition that runs through sacred text, for obvious reasons, the theme of deliverance and liberation looms large in Israel's sense of worship and covenant.

The theme of deliverance and liberation is picked up in other parts of the standard works of The Church of Jesus Christ of Latter-day Saints. I have already referenced Joseph's lament (D&C 121) as an example of Joseph crying out. Eventually, God heard that cry and Joseph's people were delivered (though, a little like Moses, Joseph never saw the people get to their final destination). Similarly, as noted earlier, Nephi (in 2 Nephi 4) lamented his weakness but was eventually freed from this burden and turned to praise and commitment. This same cycle is present in other Book of Mormon stories. As just one example, consider the story we find in Mosiah 24. In this story, the people of

FINDING NEWNESS (EVENTUALLY)

Alma (the former priest of King Noah) flee the armies of King Noah only to eventually end up in bondage to the Lamanites. Because another of Noah's former priests, Amulon, had aligned himself with the Lamanites, Alma's people were mistreated, given burdensome tasks, and forbidden to pray vocally. At this point, the scriptures record the following:

> [The people] did pour out their hearts to him [God]; and he did know the thoughts of their hearts. And it came to pass that the voice of the Lord came to them in their afflictions, saying: Lift up your heads and be of good comfort, for I know of the covenant which ye have made unto me; and I will covenant with my people and deliver them out of bondage. . . . And in the morning the Lord caused a deep sleep to come upon the Lamanites, yea, and all their task-masters were in a profound sleep. And Alma and his people departed into the wilderness. . . . [And] they poured out their thanks to God because he had been merciful unto them, and eased their burdens, and had delivered them out of bondage; for they were in bondage, and none could deliver them except it were the Lord their God. (Mosiah 24:12–13, 19–21)

Throughout Latter-day Saint scripture, we see this cycle over and over and over again: from a place of captivity/pain/anguish God's people cry out, God hears their cries, and then God takes actions to deliver/liberate them.[3]

NEWNESS AND WAITING

Lament, then, seems to be more than only a useful spiritual practice. Lament, it seems, is actually *part of the process through which* deliverance arrives. Indeed, the scriptures seem to suggest that lament and deliverance are integrally connected. Speaking specifically of Psalm 32 (referenced earlier), Brueggemann notes that "long before Freud, this psalmist understood the power of speech, the need for spoken release and admission, and the liberation that comes with the actual articulation to the one who listens and can respond."[4] Let's unpack this; Brueggemann is making a profound point. He suggests that the act of lament (the faithful articulation of our sorrow and grief to God) is a "spoken release" to the "one who listens and can respond," and that this process of release is the beginning of liberation. Israel, in crying out to God honestly, began the process of liberation; Joseph Smith, in lamenting his condition to God with faith, opened the doors of deliverance; Nephi, in lamenting his weaknesses, made himself available to being delivered from them; Alma's people, in pouring out their hearts to God, took the first step to being set free.

In a way that I am not sure anyone totally understands, lament seems to usher in deliverance. This is a paradigm-shifting insight: Deliverance and the newness it brings is *contingent upon and starts with* lament. Lament is not something that "others" who are less faithful need to go through. Rather, the cry out/God hears/deliverance sequence is *what the journey of faith looks like*.[5] I believe this is part of what Jesus was articulating when he said, "Blessed are the poor in spirit: for theirs is the kingdom of heaven. Blessed are they that mourn: for they shall be comforted" (Matthew 5:3–4). We will all be poor in spirit and we will all mourn, and, eventually, we will all be delivered.

Thus, this belief—that God will deliver us from bondage or liberate us from oppression—is the foundation upon which lament is built. Let me say that another way: because we know that God's deliverance will come (eventually), we are not afraid to honestly express to God the pain and sorrow we might feel today. This leads to a striking realization: *if we lack the faith to lament, we may also lack the faith to allow God's hand to work for our deliverance.* Or in the form of a question: How can we have faith enough to be delivered if we do not even

FINDING NEWNESS (EVENTUALLY)

have faith enough to be honest about how we feel? Lament presumes deliverance (eventually), and deliverance begins with lament. They are different sides of the same coin. Latter-day Saints believe in a God who delivers and liberates, and thus we know that we can call upon God from within our grief and sorrow. We know that when we cry out, God will hear, and we know that God will deliver us (eventually). Central to the covenant faithfulness that undergirds the Latter-day Saint tradition is trust that lament is not simply shouting into the wind, but rather that lament is followed by liberation and deliverance. Said in language that may be more common to the Latter-day Saint community: God's plan is a plan of restoration.[6]

Also, notice that in many of the experiences of deliverance previously discussed, and even in some of the personal experiences I had with lament that I shared earlier, God's work of deliverance included the participation of those being delivered. For the Israelites fleeing from Egypt, they had to actually walk out of Goshen, through the desert, and into Canaan. God could, and did, make such deliverance possible—and what God did to help deliver the people was miraculous in every sense of the word—but the Israelites had to do the walking. The same with the people of Alma being delivered from the persecution of Amulon; God created the path for deliverance by causing all of their captors to fall into a deep sleep, but Alma's people needed to wake up on time and leave while the leaving was good. The point is, as I already noted in discussing communal lament earlier, lament includes somewhere within it a call to work against the forces that cause that suffering in our own lives and in society by taking those steps that are within our power to take. By claiming our grief, pain, and sorrow and offering it to God, lament becomes a path of response and plants the seeds of action.

But I want to be clear on this point: I *am not* suggesting that we just need to pull ourselves up by our bootstraps or that if we are not delivered from suffering, the problem is that our lament is not accompanied by enough faith or dedication or hard work. Indeed, such a perspective is nothing more than an inversion of a praise-only worship paradigm and results in us viewing lament as just another variation of the "cosmic vending machine" (a perspective Elder D. Todd Christofferson counsels us to avoid). That view fundamentally misses the mark with regard to the nature of lament. Rather, I *am* suggesting that worshipping God from within our pain and sorrow is, in itself, an act of defiance against darkness and silence. Lament takes the sorrow, grief, and pain that threaten to crush us and, with a trust that can only be found in an authentic and completely open covenant relationship with God, gives those feelings and emotions to God. This kind of faithful worship, worship from within our pain, is thus a form of resistance against forces of oppression. And, eventually, when God opens the door of our deliverance, the faith upon which our acts of lament are premised is the same faith from which we find the power to walk across the threshold of newness.

LESSONS FROM HOLY SATURDAY

It is not surprising that, after walking across the threshold of newness into deliverance and liberation, God's people move from lament toward praise. That happens with the Israelites (see, for example, Exodus 15:1–18), it happens with Lehi and his family (see, for example, 1 Nephi 17:16), and it even happens in the lament psalms themselves. My sense is that it has also happened to each of us in some way or another. As we come through struggle and emerge on the other side, we desire to sing praises to God for deliverance and liberation. However, anyone who has suffered loss, disaster, or tragedy knows that it can take a long time before we feel ready to stop using the language of lament and start using the language of praise. There is a lesson in this, I think.

It seems to me that in order to embrace the newness that lament seems to invite, we must first embrace the reality that such transformation—from lament to praise, from grief and sorrow to joy, from despondence to thanksgiving—will occur on a timeline that we do not control. Returning to an image from chapter 1, in order for us to fully embrace the fact that the rain will eventually stop and that a new sunrise will eventually come, we must first embrace the reality that we cannot control how long the rain will last. Along with teaching us about the reality of deliverance, the scriptures also make clear that the movement out of loss, disaster, and tragedy will simply take the time it takes. Said another way, holding on to faith through lament will require patiently waiting. As Sue Monk Kidd observes of such waiting, "It [is]n't a matter of whether God [can] be trusted, of course, but of whether or not [we can] wait. . . . There [is] a journey to be made . . . a waiting, a gestating, a slow and uncertain birthing."[7] All newness, it seems, comes from waiting; all new life requires gestating. This waiting can be hard. It may be the hardest thing that we are asked to do. But such is the nature of the process that allows us to move into newness.

The timing of the death and resurrection of Jesus are instructive when it comes to the need to wait for newness. If we use the timing of the synoptic Gospels (Matthew 27:45–51; Luke 23:44–47; Mark 15:25),[8] Jesus was crucified around 9:00 a.m. and died about 3:00 p.m. on Friday—after the Passover meal Thursday evening but before the day of Passover ended on Friday at sunset (recall that Passover day would have started on Thursday at sunset and continued until Friday at sunset, according to how time is kept in the Jewish tradition). Christians call the Friday on which Jesus's Crucifixion occurred Good Friday. Just prior to sunset (the beginning of the Sabbath), Jesus's body was entombed, and then there followed a period of waiting.

And his followers waited for what must have felt like a very long time.

His followers did not know of Jesus's resurrection until Sunday morning (see Mark 16:2). This means that from Friday before sunset until Sunday morning—well more than twenty-four hours and closer to thirty-six hours—Jesus's believers waited in mourning and grief. Elder Jeffrey R. Holland described that period like this: "After such a short time to learn and even less time to prepare, the unthinkable happened, the unbelievable was true. Their [the Apostles'] Lord and Master, their Counselor and King, was crucified. His mortal ministry was over, and the struggling little Church He had established seemed doomed to scorn and destined for extinction."[9] This time of waiting—the Saturday between Good Friday and Easter Sunday—is called by Christians Holy Saturday.

In the chronology of Jesus's death and resurrection, Holy Saturday was the longest period of time—by a long shot. As noted above, according to the synoptic Gospels, Jesus was on the cross for about six hours. He was in the tomb for nearly thirty-six hours. This must have been an agonizing period of time for those who followed Jesus and believed in, but did not really understand, his Messianic mission. In her analysis of the Book of Mormon prophet Jacob's view of the Atonement of Jesus Christ, in particular Jacob's charge to "view" Jesus's death (Jacob 1:8), scholar Deidre Nicole Green notes, "Some Christian theologians assert that believers often move too quickly from the crucifixion to the resurrection, without adequately appreciating all that can be gleaned by reflecting upon the absence and uncertainty of what lies between Good Friday and Easter Sunday: the in-between symbolized in Holy Saturday."[10] Building on the work of Shelly Rambo—who built an entire theological framework showing the connections between trauma and the waiting Holy Saturday invites us to contemplate,[11] what Rambo calls a Theology of Remaining—Green goes on to suggest that "to view Christ's death is to remain in Christ and to remain in love, even in the uncertainty of his absence and the indefiniteness of awaiting an unrevealed future."[12] Green says that this waiting will need to occur "even in the face of uncertainty and despair."[13]

FINDING NEWNESS (EVENTUALLY)

So how can we apply the lesson of Holy Saturday to us, personally, and to the topic of lament? Many of us are (or will someday find ourselves) in the midst of a Holy Saturday in our lives. The world that we thought we knew, the hope that we thought we had, the belief that we thought we understood, or the faith upon which our life was built has been dismantled, and we have been left in uncertainty and despair. Maybe the arrival of our personal Holy Saturday happened quickly or maybe it happened slowly, but either way the result is the same: Like Jesus's followers after his death, we feel grief, sorrow, and sadness. Elder Joseph B. Wirthlin noted we all have "those days when the universe itself seems shattered and the shards of our world lie littered about us in pieces . . . those broken times when it seems we can never be put together again."[14] I have suggested that in these moments, when all else may be lost, we retain the ability to worship through lament. But lament will not immediately change things. The faith of Israel is premised on a rock-solid faith that God can and will deliver us eventually, and trust that we can indeed move from complaint to praise. But until deliverance arrives, we wait. We must simply accept the reality that "Holy Saturdays" are part of our individual and communal mortal experience, and they take as long as they take.

Often, we may be encouraged by others to move on more quickly than we should because emotions like sorrow, grief, fear, pain, and despair make those around us uncomfortable. Barbara Brown Taylor, in her meditation *Learning to Walk in the Dark*, offers us this insight: "If you have ever spent time in the company of dark emotions [such as sorrow, grief, fear, pain and despair], you too may have received the subtle messages from friends and strangers alike that you were supposed to handle them and move on sooner instead of later. Some of us have even gotten the message that if we cannot do this on a schedule, we may not have enough faith in God. If we had enough, we would be able to banish the dark angels from our bed, replacing them with the light angels of belief, trust, and praise."[15] But, as the scriptures have shown—and has been discussed throughout this book—sorrow, grief, pain, despair, and misery are not to be skipped over and avoided. Rather, they are part of a complete life. Returning to the lessons we can take from Holy Saturday, I believe that the in-between time that Holy Saturday introduced is a large part of *what makes Good Friday and Easter Sunday meaningful*. It was in the most uncertain moments of Holy Saturday when the power of Jesus's life, teachings, and death on the cross really came into focus, and it was the time of despair after his death that made the fact of his resurrection and the newness it introduced so revolutionary. In my view, not only would Jesus's atoning work have been incomplete if Holy Saturday were cut short, but our appreciation for Jesus's life and resurrection would be less profound if Holy Saturday had been preempted. As much as it may have hurt, Holy Saturday is as much a part of Jesus's Atonement (and of our personal faith journeys) as Good Friday and Easter Sunday are. Creation, joy and sorrow, death, waiting, newness. That is God's plan for all of us and for the universe.

WAITING FOR THE TURN

Elder Jeffrey R. Holland notes, "Faith means trusting God in good times and bad, even if that includes some suffering until we see His arm revealed in our behalf."[16] So how long are we to remain in this in-between place? How long will Holy Saturday last? There is just no answer that can be given. Sue Monk Kidd expresses this reality by explaining that there is a "desert that lies between our wounds and our healing, our questions and our answers, our departure and our arrival."[17] And while we are in the midst of this vast expanse of apparent emptiness, we cannot know how big that desert will be. As President Henry B. Eyring affirms, "We are [just] going to have to learn to wait upon the Lord."[18] The reality is that the Holy Saturdays of our lives will last as long as they last. In some ways, it is as painful for me to type these words as it may be for some to read them. But it is the

FINDING NEWNESS (EVENTUALLY)

truth. In my mind's eye, I can imagine someone struggling, hoping for something to help them know when the pain will stop—for a weather forecast that explains when the rain will move along so she or he will know when it is safe to finally go outside, or for a map that will lead out of the valley of the shadow of death. I can say with confidence only that God will respond in God's time. This is not waiting without hope for deliverance. In fact, as Elder Robert D. Hales taught, in the scriptures, waiting means "to hope, to anticipate, and to trust."[19] But it is also true that there are no shortcuts. Of all the truths discussed in this book, this may be the hardest. It is simply the case that the life of faith means that sometimes we have to wait. As hard as this truth may be while we are in the midst of moments of pain, this is, perhaps counterintuitively, the most important, powerful, and liberating truth we can discover: Holy Saturday will take as long as it takes.[20]

Walter Brueggemann notes that in many of the lament psalms, though the transition from lament to praise can happen from one verse to the next, we, as careful observers of life, should not let the physical proximity of the lament and praise verses fool us into believing that this transition *actually happens* so quickly in lived experience. Indeed, as President Thomas S. Monson noted, "Most of the changes [in our lives] take place subtly and slowly."[21] Yet, with reflections (especially poetic reflection like we have in the psalms or other laments), the timeline is necessarily compressed. For instance, I might reflect that it was only as I moved into adulthood that I realized the importance of reliability and discipline. Though accurate, this reflection compresses years of lived experience into a single statement. Individuals who have had similar experiences, if they take a moment to consider their own lives, will immediately recognize that there was no switch that flipped or moment of insight that suddenly and dramatically led to this growth. Rather, this transition occurred over years and years of struggles, failures, and successes. Eventually, I came to understand this fact, but this understanding was neither quickly nor painlessly achieved.

The same is true of the lament language we see in the scriptures and is true for each of us in our lives. Upon reflection—and this is played out over and over in laments—we can see how lament turns to praise. But we must not allow ourselves to forget the struggles that accompany that turn and the time that elapses. Similarly, we must not allow ourselves to forget that the process may still be ongoing and may take a very long time. To make this point, Brueggemann points to Psalm 13—a heartbreaking personal lament. The lament portion of the psalm is captured in the first four verses. They read:

> *How long, O L*ORD*? Will you forget me forever?*
> *How long will you hide your face from me?*
> *How long must I bear pain in my soul,*
> *and have sorrow in my heart all day long?*
> *How long shall my enemy be exalted over me?*
> *Consider and answer me, O L*ORD *my God!*
> *Give light to my eyes, or I will sleep the sleep of death,*
> *and my enemy will say, "I have prevailed";*
> *my foes will rejoice because I am shaken.*
>
> (P*SALM* 13:1–4, NRSV)

"Then," Brueggemann suggests, "the psalmist waits. It is a long wait in the darkness of death, a wait in disorientation. . . . There must be such a wait, perhaps a long wait, because there is no other court of appeal. One must simply wait here until there is a response."[22] We lament and then we wait. Yet, while one thing may be dying, that dying brings new birth, to paraphrase a line from a hymn sung regularly in Latter-day Saint worship services, "Upon the Cross of Calvary."[23] It is in this waiting where the ground of our lives is prepared for the growth of something new.

FINDING NEWNESS (EVENTUALLY)

THE COMING OF NEWNESS

"Newness" carries with it some interesting connotations. It suggests something that was not present before. It suggests something that did not previously exist. Out of sorrow and grief, and after waiting, we are ushered into newness. Instructively, the events surrounding Jesus's death and resurrection point to trust in newness that God's deliverance offers. As was noted earlier, in all four of the Gospels, the language Jesus uses while on the cross comes from psalms of lament. Jesus's invoking of these psalms invokes the laments the psalms contain. These laments, found in Psalms 22, 31, and 69, express feelings of grief, sorrow, abandonment, and loss. However, alongside the lament portion within each of these psalms there is *also* a turn to praise and newness. From Psalm 22, which starts with "My God, my God, why hast thou forsaken me?" we also find these statements of the anticipated deliverance and the possibility of newness that deliverance brings:

> *For he hath not despised nor abhorred the affliction of the afflicted;*
> *neither hath he hid his face from him;*
> *but when he cried unto him, he heard.*
> *My praise shall be of thee in the great congregation:*
> *I will pay my vows before them that fear him.*
> *The meek shall eat and be satisfied:*
> *they shall praise the* Lord *that seek him: your heart shall live for ever.*
> *All the ends of the world shall remember and turn unto the* Lord*:*
> *and all the kindreds of the nations shall worship before thee.*
> *For the kingdom is the* Lord*'s:*
> *and he is the governor among the nations.*

All they that be fat upon earth shall eat and worship:
 all they that go down to the dust shall bow before him:
 and none can keep alive his own soul.
A seed shall serve him;
 it shall be accounted to the Lord *for a generation.*
They shall come, and shall declare his righteousness unto a
 people that shall be born, that he hath done this.

(Psalm 22:24–31)

From Psalm 31, which contains Jesus's statement "into thine hands I commend my spirit," we find more expressions of anticipated deliverance and the possibility of newness that deliverance brings:

For I said in my haste, I am cut off from before thine eyes:
 nevertheless thou heardest the voice of my supplications
 when I cried unto thee.
O love the Lord, *all ye his saints:*
 for the Lord *preserveth the faithful. . . .*
Be of good courage, and he shall strengthen your heart, all ye
 that hope in the Lord.

(Psalm 31:22–24)

And from Psalm 69, from which Jesus's statement "I thirst" arises, we see again the promise of newness that follows the deliverance from sorrow:

I will praise the name of God with a song,
 and will magnify him with thanksgiving. . . .
The humble shall see this, and be glad:
 and your heart shall live that seek God.
For the Lord *heareth the poor,*
 and despiseth not his prisoners.
Let the heaven and earth praise him,

FINDING NEWNESS (EVENTUALLY)

> *the seas, and every thing that moveth therein.*
> *For God will save Zion, and will build the cities of Judah:*
> *that they may dwell there, and have it in possession.*
> *The seed also of his servants shall inherit it:*
> *and they that love his name shall dwell therein.*
>
> (Psalm 69:30, 32–36)

Jesus's references to these psalms—as recounted in the various Gospels—invoke the lament that each psalm contains, and each lament can inform our understanding of Jesus's suffering. Similarly, Jesus's references to these psalms *also* invokes the other half of the complaint-praise sequence that runs through the faith tradition of Israel, and thus each psalm can inform our understanding of Jesus's trust in deliverance and hope for the newness deliverance brings. Through the use of these lament psalms, Jesus cries out in an honest and authentic lament and in so doing *also* anticipates deliverance. Using the voice of complaint found in the scriptures, Jesus acknowledges a kind of death but also opens up the possibility of the coming of newness.

But to be clear, this is a turn to *newness,* not a re-turn to the past; there is no going back to the way things used to be (as anyone who has suffered true sorrow and grief will attest, going back is impossible). In fact, in returning to some of the texts that have been introduced in preceding chapters, it becomes clear that God's restorative activities are nearly always the opening of a new—often unanticipated—horizon. After all, God's plan is to help us become more than we are, not simply to take us back to where we started. But let's look at some examples.

- First, consider the newness that the Israelites experienced when they were delivered from Egypt and then from the wilderness. When the burden of servitude in Egypt caused the ancient Israelites to cry out, God did not simply re-turn them to their life in Egypt in the land of Goshen under Pharaoh's rule, where re-oppression remained a possibility. Rather, God led the Israelites into a *new* life outside of the reach of Pharaoh's oppressive policies and into a land where they could create a new covenant community based on principles that protected the weakest among them. And when the uncertainty of life in the wilderness led to petitions regarding the basic necessities of life (bread, water, and meat), God did not simply re-turn them to the subsistence lifestyle under which they had previously lived in Egypt. God, instead, introduced *new* ways of getting bread (manna), water (from a rock), and meat (quails). The experience of Israel from Egypt to Canaan was a transformational experience of newness in all aspects of life that would have been beyond the imaginative ability of this rag-tag group of formerly enslaved people.

- Consider the example of Hannah's emotional distress over her barrenness. The deliverance she experienced was not a reinsertion into her old life with less anxiety about her inability to have children. Rather, Hannah was now able to offer a prayer of thanksgiving because she had been brought into a newness of life with the birth of Samuel and five other children (see 1 Samuel 2:21). Her cup overflowed with newness.

- Consider the example of Alma's people suffering under the persecution of Amulon. When the weight of Amulon's tactics were more than Alma's people could bear, God did not re-turn them to their former life. That is to say, God did not simply wind back the clock to a time before the oppressive policies of Amulon began. Rather, God led Alma's people into a new life and a new community where they flourished. The experience of Alma's people was not a re-turn to the past but a dramatic new future with new opportunities.

- Consider the example of Jeremiah, whose deliverance took on a very different character from that of the Israelites leaving bondage in Egypt or Alma being led away from Amulon's persecution. As noted above, Jeremiah—the outsider from Anathoth—witnessed the destruction of his people and the desecration of Israel's most holy site. Though the exiles were eventually restored to the land and the temple was rebuilt, he did not live long enough to see it. The laments attributed to Jeremiah, which we examined in part earlier, are a devastatingly honest cry of anguish. It is hard to imagine coming back from such tragedy. However, this same Jeremiah, whose heart was torn open in sorrow, also offered remarkably optimistic and hopeful words of encouragement to those who were in exile in Babylon. Even though he saw the slow-motion destruction of Jerusalem at the hands of the Babylonians, Jeremiah suggested that the exiles in Babylon "build houses and live in them; plant gardens and eat what they produce. Take wives and have sons and daughters; take wives for your sons, and give your daughters in marriage . . . ; multiply there. . . . seek the welfare of the city" (Jeremiah 29:5–7, NRSV).[24] What a remarkable turn. Jeremiah mourned; and Jeremiah could also see new beginnings on the horizon.[25]

With those scriptural examples as a backdrop, let's now consider some of the laments that we have looked at previously: Psalms 6, 13, 44, 74, 79 (perhaps take a moment to reread the lament portion of those psalms). Each of them has a turn to newness.

The LORD hath heard my supplication;
the LORD will receive my prayer.

(PSALM 6:9)

But I trusted in your steadfast love;
my heart shall rejoice in your salvation.
I will sing to the LORD,
because he has dealt bountifully with me.

(PSALM 13:5–6, NRSV)

Thou art my King, O God. . . .
Thou hast saved us from our enemies. . . .
In God we boast all the day long, and praise thy name for ever.
(PSALM 44:4, 7–8)

*For God is my King of old, working salvation in the midst of
   the earth.*
(PSALM 74:12)

*So we thy people and sheep of thy pasture will give thee thanks
   for ever:
   we will shew forth thy praise to all generations.*
(PSALM 79:13)

Recall that each of the statements of praise above is found in the same psalms that also articulated heart-wrenching expressions of grief and sorrow. Within the self-same psalms, the psalmists move from lament to praise. And many of these expressions of trust in God's deliverance have a component of praise that is expressly *forward-looking* and *anticipating a newness that has not yet arrived*. We do not know how long the psalmist had to wait before being able to move from lament and to praise. Maybe it was a long time, or maybe it happened quickly. But it happened, eventually. Perhaps like Jeremiah, in unburdening themselves of their grief and sorrow through lament, the psalmists make room to see the possibilities of newness.

Finally, and powerfully, Jesus's actual resurrection embodies the newness to which lament seems to point. Jesus's death was a death, real and final. Jesus died. And resurrection did not bring Jesus "back" to his previous earthly life. Jesus's resurrection did not "undo" his death; he did not return to the mortal experience he'd had prior to the Crucifixion. Far from it, in fact. Jesus's resurrection, which came out of his death, ushered in something entirely *new*. Jesus's deliverance from the tomb was not a return to the past, but a full *re-creation*.

Jesus's resurrection (deliverance) ushered into this mortal plain a new kind of life.

Elder Robert D. Hales reminds us that "out of suffering, sorrow, and sadness . . . joy will come."[26] This is the faith tradition that Latter-day Saints have inherited. This confidence in newness—the anticipation of deliverance—is the lifeblood of the gospel of Jesus Christ. Elder Joseph B. Wirthlin summed up this reality in three powerful words: "Sunday *will* come."[27] And, in ways that are too often overlooked, this movement toward newness is grounded in the same covenant commitment from which lament springs. It is in this way that lament and the coming of newness are intricately and inextricably connected. Lament, and all it entails (faithfulness, holding on, honest and authentic worship, patience, etc.), is a step toward deliverance, and the newness that deliverance ushers in is more remarkable than can be imagined—it will be an extraordinary newness; it is truly *deliverance*.

ON REMEMBERING

Perhaps unexpectedly, the newness of deliverance does not erase the memory of the suffering from which lament originates, it does not cause us to forget the uncertainty we felt while we were waiting, and it does not rub away the footprints we left along the long road to deliverance. Loss is still loss, disaster is still disaster, and tragedy is still tragedy. Tears may be wiped away, but a memory of crying remains. The newness of deliverance is not a cure that makes life's challenges magically disappear, nor does it purge them from our own book of life. As noted earlier, Job was delivered from his trials and moved into newness—new health, a bigger family, and additional riches—but the recollection of his previous loss likely never left. He must have remembered the children who had died and the flocks for which he had cared. Newness is not escapism. In fact, the reality of remembering our situation before deliverance and the painful process through which we passed seems to be a critical part of our faith journey and a necessary element to embracing the newness of deliverance. The importance of remembering previous struggles is scattered throughout the standard works; however, I will focus on two specific instances that speak to me personally. That said, there are many other examples where the faithful are encouraged to remember their deliverance; Elder Dale G. Renlund, for instance, points to the example of Alma the Younger, whose recollection of his own suffering and subsequent deliverance provided a powerful teaching tool for others.[28] By recalling deliverance, we are able to see the newness as the unexpected miracle that it is.

As a first example on the importance of remembering, recall the earlier discussion of the Israelites' Exodus from Egypt. Once enslaved under the harsh hand of Pharaoh and then later hungry and thirsty in the wilderness, God's deliverance led the Israelites out of bondage and out of hunger and thirst and into the newness of manna, water from a rock, and quail, and then into a land with vineyards and olive groves already planted (see Joshua 24:13) where they could build a community based on God's vision for humanity and free from forced labor and oppressive policies. And yet, throughout this journey from oppression to newness, from lament to praise, the Israelites are told more times than I could count to remember their time in Egypt. "Remember," says God, "that you were enslaved in Egypt" (see Deuteronomy 15:15; 24:18). And why? There are at least two reasons according to our sacred text:

First, the scriptures suggest on the one hand that this remembering fosters the extension of that newness to others. The Israelites are commanded: "If a member of your community, whether a Hebrew man or a Hebrew woman, is sold[29] to you and works for you six years, in the seventh year you shall set that person free. And when you send a male slave [or servant] out from you a free person, you shall not send him out empty-handed. Provide liberally out of your flock, your threshing floor, and your wine press, thus giving to him some of the bounty with which the LORD your God has blessed you. Remember that you were a slave in the land of Egypt, and the LORD your God redeemed you; for this reason I lay this command upon you today" (Deuteronomy 15:13–15, NRSV). The point here seems to be that as the Israelites remember their own deliverance and recognize the place of newness in which they now reside, they are better able to bring that newness—the liberation from oppression that they had experienced—to others. God's deliverance for the Israelites becomes a virtuous cycle. The Israelites are to reenact, for others, the deliverance that they themselves had experienced. By recalling their deliverance, the Israelites change the way they treat those around them. Moreover, because the Israelites remembered what it is like to be enslaved, they were in a position to identify with all those who were suffering under this yoke as well—they are in a position to practice communal lament.

Second, this "remembering" of a pre-deliverance life ensures that the miracle of newness remains present in the lives of the Israelites. As the Israelites remember their former situation, they are better able to continually recognize the newness in which they reside. In remembering enslavement, the newness of deliverance remains in their immediate field of vision. Said differently, without remembering their "old life," their newness might eventually be experienced as the status quo and lead to a new kind of oppression. Because of their experience as an enslaved people, and because of their deliverance, the Israelites are specially equipped to appreciate the newness they are experiencing and to introduce a new way of being into the world that avoids the types of activities from which deliverance was needed. Newness begets newness.

As a second example on the importance of remembering, in Doctrine and Covenants 19 we have a revelation through which Jesus recalls the suffering he endured during his atoning work. It is clear from his description that the details of those moments remain clear in Jesus's mind and body. In verses 16 and 18, Jesus's voice is in the first person, and we get an intimate description of these events: "I, God, have suffered these things. . . . Which suffering caused myself, even God, the greatest of all, to tremble because of pain, and to bleed at every pore, and to suffer both body and spirit." These statements make clear that Jesus did not forget this suffering. In fact, it is interesting that the description found in section 19 is entirely composed in the past tense—it is a reflection on the past. These statements are expressly framed as an act of remembering. Further, we know that Jesus carries (even now) the marks of the cross in his hands, feet, and side—constant physical reminders of his suffering (see John 20:27; 3 Nephi 11:14). But Jesus does not seem to find these acts of remembering a hindrance to the newness that came following his resurrection. Rather, the deliverance he experienced (and that he ushers in for all of us) *enfolds* his suffering. Jesus's suffering has become *part of* his newness.

Think about that for a moment: Jesus's suffering is part of his newness. The reasons for this are similar to the situation of the Israelites described earlier. Because Jesus can recall his suffering from his place of newness, Jesus is specially equipped to help others who are suffering and bring them into newness alongside him. Jesus's ability to remember his life experience, including specifically suffering, is central to continuing atoning work. This connection is made explicit in the Book of Mormon. Alma describes Jesus's "bowels to be filled with mercy," enabling him to "know according to the flesh how to succor his people according to their infirmities." Jesus can do this perfectly because he recalls the "pains and afflictions and temptations of every kind" which he experienced (Alma 7:11, 13). The Atonement of Jesus is many things, but it certainly includes this reality: Jesus, even in his exalted newness, can fully identify with us in our moments of sorrow, and because Jesus has walked that path himself and remembers what it was like, he can walk with us into the newness he offers.

These two examples, when taken together, give us a key to better understanding the somewhat perplexing response Joseph Smith received to his lament in Doctrine and Covenants 121. As part of God's response to Joseph's plea, "O God, where art thou?" (D&C 121:1), Joseph was told that suffering would continue for a time and was given this insight: "Know thou, my son, that all these things shall give thee experience, and shall be for thy good" (D&C 122:7). How can that be? I think that God was helping Joseph understand that life is a continual process of moving through sadness and grief and into praise and deliverance. But the newness that God has in store (for Joseph and for us) is not a paradisiacal obliviousness where all of the painful experiences of life are fully expunged from our memory, but rather a transformation of what is into what could be. What God seemed to be teaching Joseph is that worshipping through lament—holding on to a covenant relationship in the midst of sorrow, loss, disaster, or tragedy—leads, eventually, to an entirely new re-creation, to a new way of being for ourselves and our communities. The relational foundations upon which the ability to worship through lament rests are the same foundations of faith through which creation is restored.

The implications of this reality are powerful. As was noted at the beginning of this book, sadness, grief, and sorrow are not only part of life but also a vital component of the plan of salvation. We *need* sadness, grief, and sorrow. These experiences are for our good. Not because suffering is inherently good or godly. In fact, I want to avoid diligently the suggestion that all suffering, specifically that which is unearned, is intended by God to occur or, even worse, a perverse indication of divine favor. The brief discussion on theodicy from earlier observes that attributing all suffering to God is a fraught proposition. Rather, there is something about sadness, grief, and sorrow—which we will inevitably encounter—that has the potential to open us up to newness. Elder Neal A. Maxwell affirmed this reality when he noted, "Much as I lament the gathering storms, there will be some usefulness in them."[30] Sue Monk Kidd expressed this same sentiment by observing, "Growth germinates not in tent dwelling but in upheaval."[31] God seems to know that, left to our own devices, most of us would be content to avoid sorrow, grief, and pain. But in avoiding misery, as Lehi explains, we would also avoid joy. What's more, by avoiding sadness, grief, and sorrow, we would never experience the newness that deliverance ushers in. Without Pharaoh, there is no Exodus; without the wilderness there is no manna; without the cross there is no empty tomb. This is the great alchemy of God's grace. Deliverance from loss, disaster, or tragedy is not a return to life "before," but rather a passageway into a new life that is more remarkable than the life we had previously imagined.[32] Put bluntly: "There is no newness unless and until there is a serious death of the old."[33] Lament is the epicenter of this transformational process. Lament is how we hold on to covenants from within the storm and how we claim our experience for God. Lament is a necessary component of enfolding the totality of our lives into the rubric of sacred worship.

NEWNESS, RE-CREATION, AND RESTORATION

The gospel message of the Latter-day Saints is imbued with the language of restoration. Not surprisingly, this vision has its roots deep in the Old and New Testaments. Ancient prophets like Isaiah, Ezekiel, and Malachi spoke movingly of Israel's return from a life of exile into a new life; one that would be more remarkable than that which preceded exile (for example, see Isaiah 48:8–16; Ezekiel 36:16–38; Malachi 4:4–6).[34] The New Testament asserts that newness can only come as old things pass away, thereby preparing the ground for all things to become new (see 2 Corinthians 5:17). And in our time, Elder Dieter F. Uchtdorf has spoken of "the magnificent gift of new opportunity, new life, new hope" as part of our "daily restoration."[35] More than just a return to things as they used to be, restoration in the Latter-day Saint context is actually more synonymous with the idea of re-creation. Just as Jesus's resurrection was the introduction of a new kind of life (not a resumption of his old life), Latter-day Saints' faith includes the anticipation of a new heaven and a new earth. It includes the anticipation of new bodies and new opportunities for development and growth. And in these contexts, "new" does not mean a return to what was, but the re-creation of what *is* into a coming newness of what *could be*.[36] For Latter-day Saints, the restoration of all things really means the re-creation of all things into a newness that is grander than we can imagine.

Within the context of this discussion on lament, the restoration worldview has individual and institutional reverberations. From an individual perspective, we should expect that restoration—the bringing of newness—will require what Elder Neal A. Maxwell calls "God's stretching."[37] "Sooner or later," Barbara Brown Taylor suggests, "you will have to leave all your soothing props behind, entrusting yourself to the God who cares more about your transformation than your comfort."[38] Without lament we are holding something back. Individually, we must be willing to leave behind the "soothing props" of praise-only language and embrace the authenticity of lament when the situation calls for it. Exaltation demands nothing less. From a community perspective, the restoration worldview requires the continual renewal of our community and the communities with which we interact. This means that: (1) alongside other Christian denominations, we must create room for lament. As one commentator notes of Christianity generally, but I believe this applies to the Church of Jesus Christ as well, "We must seek to be the church that integrates the theology of suffering with the theology of celebration. We must seek to be the church that engages in both praise and lament. We must seek to be the church that embodies the full narrative of Christ in his suffering and in his triumph. Lament offers us a glimpse of what we must seek."[39] Further, along with making theological space for the language of lament, we need to (2) continue to develop a culture that, through communal lament, is both more aware of and more actively seeks to remedy the suffering and sorrow that is so present in the world, and especially that suffering and sorrow for which we may be responsible. Certainly, there is movement in this direction, but there is also more that could be done.

Abraham Heschel observes that "life is a response, not a soliloquy."[40] In this brief observation, Heschel uncovers one of the great truths of our existence. Life is meant to be a dialogue with God, not a speech we make on our own or a sermon by God to which we passively listen. But such dialogues can only be transformative to the degree that they are truly open and uninhibited. When we hold something back, we stall our own progression toward becoming new creatures (see 2 Corinthians 5:17). Just like the language of praise frames critical components of our Christian vocation, so too the language of lament teaches us what it means to be a Christian. Creation is on its way to being transformed. Lament is part of that transformation. Latter-day Saints believe in a God who listens and hears. Do we have the faith to speak honestly? Latter-day Saints have confidence in a God that delivers. Are we willing to exercise the "risky faith" of lament that a truly authentic relationship with God requires, and can we recognize and grieve with those for whom praise-only worship is not yet a possibility? Latter-day Saints embrace the restoration of all things. Will we let lament take us there?

EPILOGUE

A BRIEF WORD ON LAMENT AND "FAITH CRISIS"

Our individual faith journeys are (and should be) dynamic, and they incorporate an ongoing, intentional, continual revisiting of our own taken-for-granted assumptions, ideas, and beliefs. Recently, Elder Jeffrey R. Holland even noted that "real faith—life-changing faith, Abrahamic faith—is always in crisis. That's how you find out if it's faith at all."[1] Our God is the God of growth and progress. However, the development of life-changing faith can be painful at times and stretch us to our limits. And that is especially true when the challenges we face in our faith journey come, in some way or another, from *within* our faith community. Lately, these kinds of challenges have been called a "faith crisis."

Yet, in my view, the notion of a "faith crisis" is neither very precise nor very accurate. Depending on the person, "faith crisis" could mean variously "faith loss" or "faith rebuilding" or "loss of trust" or "disillusionment" or "transition of belief" or "acceptance of new ideas" or "faith maturation" or myriad other things. Thus, the language of "faith crisis" seems to me to be too broad to be very useful because it ignores the radical uniqueness of each person's life experience. What's more, I think the language of "faith crisis" can be damaging inasmuch as it is used to suggest a "faith crisis" can be avoided by deepened ideological retrenchment.

Challenges with the phrase aside, the increased usage of the term does seem to point to the demographic reality that some of the

Latter-day Saints' best and brightest have decided to no longer align themselves with this faith community. The reasons for which individuals disassociate themselves with the Latter-day Saint community are as varied and individual as the people themselves.[2] For some it may be unease with points of doctrine, for others it might be concern with specific Church policies, and for some it could be the result of terribly unfortunate interactions with ecclesiastical leaders. Or it might be something else.[3] In some instances, individuals may feel that because the challenge they face originates from within the Church, leaving is the only option remaining. However, in my view, that need not be the inevitable outcome of grappling with faith—even when the points of concern center around or come from within the Latter-day Saint tradition. In fact, as Elder Jeffrey R. Holland seems to suggest in the quote at the beginning of this section, such tumult might in fact be an avenue to a newness of faith. And this turn to newness often begins with lament. It is for this reason that I believe a deeper embrace of lament as a resource in the Latter-day Saint worship community could be a valuable tool for those who are in the midst of a restructuring of their faith. Let me explain.

When Church members react with grief, sorrow, sadness, or even outrage to doctrinal, historical, or policy concerns, or to unfortunate interactions with ecclesiastical leaders (or to whatever is the source of their grief and sorrow)—all of which are reasonable, human reactions; in many instances these types of challenges-from-within upend someone's worldview—too often the counsel offered is the functional equivalent of an ultimatum: choose faithfulness and stay, or choose faithlessness and leave. In saying this, I realize it is likely not presented this starkly (or I hope it is not), but for those in the midst of a faith-storm, advice like, "Just keep coming to church" and "Follow the prophet even if you are not sure" can certainly feel like a dismissal of someone's concern. For some, it may be difficult to keep coming to church when it is the actions of an ecclesiastical leader in a specific

A BRIEF WORD ON LAMENT AND "FAITH CRISIS"

ward or stake that is the source of their pain. For others, it might be challenging to follow the current prophet when the things prophets have said or done in the past are the cause of their sorrow. To label someone's grief, sorrow, sadness, or outrage as "faithlessness" fundamentally misses the mark in my view because it (1) presumes that one cannot be faithful from within grief, sorrow, sadness, and outrage, and then (2) silences and marginalizes those who may be most in need of worshipping with the language that lament provides.

I believe that Latter-day Saints equipped with the ability to lament have at the ready a powerful resource for handling the loss, disaster, and tragedy we experience in our faith journeys. Lament gives us a way to faithfully remain in a covenant relationship with God even in the midst of expressing our sorrow, grief, and sadness over a specific incident, event, policy, or doctrine. Lament gives us a way to speak authentically to God even if pillars of our faith crash down. Further, when our community makes more space for lament, we also make more space for those individuals who need to express lament to continue to worship with us. That is to say, by embracing lament, we create space for people to express their grief, sorrow, sadness, and outrage without feeling like they have to leave our community to voice those feelings.

Similarly, when it comes to more existential questions (Are God and Jesus real? Does all of this actually matter? Is there a reason for life?)—many of which are brought on by loss, tragedy, or disaster of some sort—lament can be a tool for remaining in dialogue with the Divine when other forms of communication are no longer possible. As is made expressly clear in the discussion earlier, lament does not resolve life's challenges, nor does it answer life's questions. Lament is a way to mourn a loss, protest a tragedy, or process a disaster. In this way, lament can help us explore the depths of divine silence that is characteristic of these moments in life. Returning again to the wisdom of Barbara Brown Taylor, she observes that "by addressing the experience of God's silence . . . in our [own] lives, we may be able to open up the possibility that silence is as much a sign of God's presence as of God's absence—the divine silence is not a vacuum to be filled but a mystery to be entered into, unarmed with words and undistracted by noise—a holy of holies in which we too may be struck dumb by the power of the unsayable God."[4] Similarly, Michael Card asserts, "Lament is the path that takes us to the place where we discover that there is no complete answer to pain and suffering, only Presence."[5] Sometimes, sensing the reality of a divine presence is answer enough, and I think lament is one way that this can happen.

To be clear, I am not suggesting that the goal of lament is to maintain or increase Church membership or to prevent people from transitioning to an entirely new way of relating to God and the world. What I am suggesting is that in those moments when our road of faith may feel blocked, lament is a lifeline to which we or our friends can cling. Lament is a tool in the toolbox to foster authentic, covenant relationships when all the other tools seem to stop working. There is nothing faithless about clinging to covenant through lament. In fact, it is the ability—individually and communally—to worship from within our sorrow, grief, and sadness that creates the conditions from which we can anticipate deliverance and see the possibility of newness in our lives, our communities, our institutions, and our world. Lament is the catalyst of change. And that newness that deliverance offers is something we can scarcely imagine.

NOTES

CHAPTER 1

1. See Pew Research Center, "Religion's Relationship to Happiness, Civic Engagement and Health Around the World," Jan. 31, 2019.
2. Pew Research Center, "Religious Landscape Study," 2014.
3. I recognize that not all Utahns are members of (or active in) the Church and that not all Church members live in Utah. However, for the purpose of looking at general statistics, Utah's rates for suicide, depression, and anxiety are one of the few indicators available. There is a dearth of reliable statistics that examine these factors as a function of region across states or countries.
4. Sharecare, "Community Well-Being Index," https://wellbeingindex.sharecare.com/, accessed December 2, 2021.
5. *Teachings of the Presidents of the Church: Gordon B. Hinckley* (2016), 69–79.
6. *Teachings of the Presidents of the Church: Gordon B. Hinckley*, 74.
7. Russell M. Nelson, "Joy and Spiritual Survival," *Ensign*, November 2016.
8. Rachel Sterzer Gibson, "Latter-day Saint youth and suicide: What to know and how to help," *Church News*, September 2, 2021.
9. Centers for Disease Control and Prevention, National Center for Health Statistics, "Anxiety and Depression, Household Pulse Survey," https://www.cdc.gov/nchs/covid19/pulse/mental-health.htm.
10. Jane Clayson Johnson, *Silent Souls Weeping* (Salt Lake City: Deseret Book, 2018).
11. Barbara Brown Taylor, *Learning to Walk in the Dark* (New York: HarperOne, 2014), 134.
12. Jeffrey R. Holland, "Like a Broken Vessel," *Ensign*, November 2013.
13. Robert D. Hales, "Your Sorrow Shall Be Turned to Joy," *Ensign*, November 1983.
14. This is a temptation to which Job's friends succumbed and for which they were rightly chastised (see Job 42:7).
15. Walter Brueggemann, *The Message of the Psalms* (Minneapolis, MN: Augsburg Publishing, 1984), 51.
16. William Goldman, *The Princess Bride, 30th Anniversary Edition* (New York: Random House, 2003), 144.
17. *The Good Place*, "Existential Crisis," Season 2, Episode 4, Beth McCarty-Miller (director), aired October 12, 2017.

NOTES

CHAPTER 2

1. Kate Bowler, *Everything Happens for a Reason and Other Lies I've Loved* (New York: Random House, 2019), 25, 26.
2. Kate Bowler, *Everything Happens for a Reason and Other Lies I've Loved*, 26.
3. D. Todd Christofferson, "Our Relationship with God," *Liahona*, May 2022.
4. Adele Berlin and Marc Zvi Brettler, ed., *The Jewish Study Bible, 2nd edition* (New York: Oxford University Press, 2014), 1581. This is the first word of the book of Lamentations in Hebrew.
5. The title *Koheleth* is translated as "teacher" in a variety of English translations of the Bible. The New Jewish Publication Society's translation of the Hebrew Bible uses this transliteration of the underlying Hebrew and notes that this title likely references something like "the Assembler," i.e. the assembler of the wisdom and sayings found in this collection. See Adele Berlin and Marc Zvi Brettler, ed., *The Jewish Study Bible*, 1602, fn *a*.
6. Though I will not explore this notion more deeply here, I owe the insight about how Enoch's vision shows the possibility of God to Terryl and Fiona Givens, who have written beautifully on this subject. See, for instance, Fiona and Terryl Givens, *The Christ Who Heals: How God Restored the Truth That Saves Us* (Salt Lake City: Deseret Book, 2017), 94; and Terryl Givens, *Wrestling the Angel* (England: Oxford University Press, 2015), 84–89.
7. Amy-Jill Levine and Marc Zvi Brettler, *The Bible With and Without Jesus* (New York: HarperOne, 2020), 365.
8. Jeffrey R. Holland, "None Were with Him," *Ensign*, April 2009.
9. Barbara Brown Taylor, *When God Is Silent* (Norwich, England: Canterbury Press, 2013), 78.
10. Jeffrey R. Holland, "Waiting on the Lord," *Ensign*, November 2020.
11. Soong-Chan Rah, *Prophetic Lament, A Call for Justice in Troubled Times* (Downers Grove, IL: IVP Books, 2015), 47.
12. Michael Card, *A Sacred Sorrow, Reaching Out to God in the Lost Language of Lament* (Colorado Springs, CO: NavPress, 2005), 21.

A BRIEF DIVERSION ON THE GENRE OF LAMENT

1. Thank you to my good friend Eric Lacey, who rightly suggested that making this distinction was important.
2. Neal A. Maxwell, "Murmur Not," *Ensign*, November 1989.
3. Neal A. Maxwell, "Murmur Not."
4. *Come, Follow Me—For Individuals and Families: Old Testament 2022* (2021).
5. Walter Brueggemann, *The Message of the Psalms* (Minneapolis: Augsburg Publishing, 1984), 173.
6. John Hilton III, "Old Testament Psalms in the Book of Mormon," in *Ascending the Mountain of the Lord: Temple, Praise, and Worship in the Old Testament* (2013 Sperry Symposium), ed. Jeffrey R. Chadwick, Matthew J. Grey, and David Rolph Seely

(Provo, UT: Religious Studies Center, Brigham Young University; Salt Lake City: Deseret Book, 2013), 306.
7. See, for instance, *The Rule of St. Benedict*, Carolinne White, trans. (London: Penguin Classics, 2008), which was originally written in the mid-sixth century CE, and is just one of many monastic "rules" that outlined which psalms were to be recited at which times.
8. This type of approach, called a form criticism, seeks to understand the psalms based on their structure and the context in which they might have been used. Foundational form-critical analyses of the Psalter include Claus Westerman, *The Psalms: Structure, Content, and Message*, trans. Ralph D. Gehrke (Minneapolis: Augsburg Publishing House, 1980); Walter Brueggemann, *The Message of the Psalms* (Minneapolis: Augsburg Publishing, 1984); Hermann Gunkel, *Introduction to the Psalm: The Genres of Religious Lyric of Israel*, trans. James D. Nogalski (Macon, GA: Mercer Press, 1998).
9. Soong-Chan Rah, *Prophetic Lament, A Call for Justice in Troubled Times* (Downers Grove, IL: IVP Books, 2015), 44.
10. This framing—articulation to submission to relinquishment—comes from Walter Brueggemann's "The Costly Loss of Lament," in Patrick D. Miller, ed., *The Psalms and the Life of Faith* (Minneapolis: Fortress Press, 1995), 100.
11. Denise Dombkowski Hopkins, *Journey Through the Psalms, Revised and Expanded* (St. Louis: Chalice Press, 2002), 82.
12. Denise Dombkowski Hopkins, *Journey Through the Psalms*, 82.
13. Michael Card, *A Sacred Sorrow: Reaching Out to God in the Lost Language of Lament* (Colorado Springs, CO: NavPress, 2005), 129.

CHAPTER 3

1. Abraham Joshua Heschel, *God in Search of Man* (New York: FSG Books, 1976), 119.
2. See Dean M. Davies, "The Blessings of Worship," *Ensign*, November 2016.
3. Walter Brueggemann, "The Costly Loss of Lament," in Patrick D. Miller, ed., *The Psalms and the Life of Faith* (Minneapolis: Fortress Press, 1995), 102.
4. Michael Card, *A Sacred Sorrow: Reaching Out to God in the Lost Language of Lament* (Colorado Springs, CO: NavPress, 2005), 29.
5. Michael Card, *A Sacred Sorrow*, 137.
6. Denise Dombkowski Hopkins, *Journey Through the Psalms, Revised and Expanded* (St. Louis: Chalice Press, 2002), 119.
7. Denise Dombkowski Hopkins, *Journey Through the Psalms*, 119.
8. Denise Dombkowski Hopkins, *Journey Through the Psalms*, 119.
9. Walter Brueggemann, *Praying the Psalms* (Eugene, OR: Cascade Books, 2007), 10–11.
10. Denise Dombkowski Hopkins, *Journey Through the Psalms*, 96.
11. See, for instance, "Visiting Teaching Message: Participate in Sincere Prayer," *Liahona*, June 2009; J. Devn Cornish, "The Privilege of Prayer," *Ensign*, November 2011.
12. Walter Brueggemann, *The Message of the Psalms* (Minneapolis: Augsburg Publishing, 1984), 97.
13. Walter Brueggemann, *The Message of the Psalms*, 79; emphasis added.
14. Neal A. Maxwell, "Apply the Atoning Blood of Christ," *Ensign*, November 1997.
15. Walter Brueggemann, *The Message of the Psalms*, 52.

NOTES

CHAPTER 4

1. Jeffrey R. Holland, "Look to God and Live," *Ensign*, November 1993.
2. In my limited experience, *Shoah* is commonly favored over Holocaust in texts written by Jewish authors, hence my use of the term here. However, for a thoughtful discussion about the relative strengths and weaknesses of these and other word-choice options, see Rabbi Wayne Allen, *Thinking about Good and Evil: Jewish Views from Antiquity to Modernity* (Philadelphia: Jewish Publication Society, 2021), 273–76.
3. Michael Card, *A Sacred Sorrow: Reaching Out to God in the Lost Language of Lament* (Colorado Springs, CO: NavPress, 2005), 28.
4. Consistent with tradition, including biblical traditions that seem to point to Jeremiah as a composer of laments (2 Chronicles 35:25), I am taking Jeremiah as the author of Lamentations for the purposes of this discussion. Even if not authored by Jeremiah, the larger point about how laments can serve as faithful worship remains true.
5. Amy-Jill Levine and Marc Zvi Brettler, *The Bible With and Without Jesus* (New York: HarperOne, 2020), 359.
6. Amy-Jill Levine and Marc Zvi Brettler, *The Bible With and Without Jesus*, 359.
7. Jo Ann Hackett, "1 and 2 Samuel," in Carol A. Newsom, et al., ed., *Women's Bible Commentary, 20th Anniversary Edition* (Louisville, KY: Westminster Press, 2012), 153–54. In addition to the obvious social and religious implications of barrenness that may have compelled Hannah to seek a child, Hackett also notes that Hannah's approach—offering the "first fruits" of her childbearing to YHWH—is "in hopes of receiving more children in return" (154).
8. Generally, biblical scholarship sees the prophetic tradition beginning with Samuel. In the Old Testament, prophets usually arise as a counterbalance to Israel's (and later Israel's and Judah's) kings, serving as an antagonist to royal power. Samuel was the first to serve this role, hence the reason he is identified as the first in this tradition. In the Latter-day Saint tradition, the term *prophet* is more general and not necessarily bound to the notion of counterbalancing political actors.
9. Scholars note anachronisms in Hannah's prayer, specifically in verse 10, which says that "the Lord . . . will give strength to his king" (NRSV). There was no king in Israel at the time Hannah prayed. This likely indicates that some portions of the psalm were written later and then added at some point. This type of editing/insertion is unremarkable; it is common across the Old Testament and, in fact, throughout all of the standard works. All of the Latter-day Saint sacred texts have undergone changes and editing. The presence of such editing does not impact the point here, which is the recognition of a spoken prayer and a discussion of how the use of a psalm played a role in that.
10. Walter Brueggemann, "The Costly Loss of Lament," in Patrick D. Miller, ed., *The Psalms and the Life of Faith* (Minneapolis: Fortress Press, 1995), 99.
11. Amy-Jill Levine and Marc Zvi Brettler, *The Bible With and Without Jesus*, 360.
12. Denise Dombkowski Hopkins, *Journey Through the Psalms, Revised and Expanded* (St. Louis: Chalice Press, 2002), 113. Quoting Ulrike Bail, "O God Hear My Prayer: Psalm 55 and Violence against Women," in *Wisdom and Psalms: A Feminist Companion to the Bible* (2nd series), Athalya Brenner and Carole Fontaine, ed. (Sheffield, England: Sheffield Academic Press, 1998), 127–28.

NOTES

13. Russell M. Nelson, "Revelation for the Church, Revelation for our Lives," *Ensign*, May 2018.
14. See Biblehub's entry on *tseaqah* (Strong's Concordance, word number 6818) as one location, among many, where Strong's Concordance can be accessed (https://biblehub.com/hebrew/6818.htm).
15. Interestingly, this Greek word is also attributed to Stephen in his description of the Israelites' deliverance from Pharaoh. Stephen paraphrases Exodus 3:7 thusly: "I have seen, I have seen the affliction of my people which is in Egypt, and I have heard their groaning, and am come down to deliver them" (Acts 7:34). In this verse, *stenagmos* is also the Greek word translated as "groaning." See Biblehub's entry on *stenagmos* (Strong's Concordance, word number 4726) as one location, among many, where Strong's Concordance can be accessed (https://biblehub.com/greek/4726.htm).
16. Gustavo Gutierrez, *On Job* (Maryknoll, NY: Orbis Books, 1970), 101.
17. Walter Brueggemann, *The Message of the Psalms* (Minneapolis: Augsburg Publishing, 1984), 52.
18. Walter Brueggemann, "The Costly Loss of Lament," 104.
19. Michael Card, *A Sacred Sorrow*, 30.
20. See "Doctrine and Covenants, 1844," p. 69, The Joseph Smith Papers, accessed January 5, 2022, https://www.josephsmithpapers.org/paper-summary/doctrine-and-covenants-1844/71. The original quote is, "A religion that does not require the sacrifice of all things, never has the power sufficient to produce the faith necessary unto life and salvation."

CHAPTER 5

1. Kate Bowler, *Everything Happens for a Reason and Other Lies I've Loved* (New York: Random House, 2019), 170–72.
2. Walter Brueggemann, *Praying the Psalms* (Eugene, OR: Cascade Books, 2007), 21.
3. The Hebrew word that is often translated as "holy" or "sacred" is the word *qodesh*, according to Strong's Concordance. The word connotes a thing (or place) that is dedicated to or consecrated for God (as in Numbers 31:6; 35:25; Deuteronomy 26:13; Joshua 5:15; 6:19; 1 Samuel 21:7; 2 Kings 12:4, 18; 1 Chronicles 4:49; 9:49, etc.). See Biblehub's entry on *qodesh* (Strong's Concordance, word number 6944) as one location where Strong's Concordance can be accessed (https://biblehub.com/hebrew/strongs_6944.htm).
4. John Henry Newman, "The Pillar and the Cloud," in *Lead, Kindly Light: Meditations, Poems, and Prayers for the Journey*, vol. 1 (Acropolis Scholars, 2019), 12.
5. Emma Lou Thayne, "Where Can I Turn for Peace?," *Hymns* (1985), no. 129.
6. "Sometimes I Feel Like a Motherless Child," Hymnary (website), https://hymnary.org/text/sometimes_i_feel_like_a_motherless_child.
7. Denise Dombkowski Hopkins, *Journey Through the Psalms, Revised and Expanded* (St. Louis: Chalice Press, 2002), 11.

NOTES

CHAPTER 6

1. Daniel Belnap, "A Comparison of the Communal Lament Psalms and the Treaty-Covenant Formula," *Studies in the Bible and Antiquity*, vol. 1 (2009), 34; emphasis added.
2. "People and Poverty," *The World Counts* (website), accessed Jan. 8, 2022, https://www.theworldcounts.com/challenges/people-and-poverty/hunger-and-obesity/how-many-people-die-from-hunger-each-year/story. See also "Losing 25,000 to Hunger Every Day," *The UN Chronicle*, accessed Jan. 8, 2022, https://www.un.org/en/chronicle/article/losing-25000-hunger-every-day.
3. Walter Brueggemann, *The Message of the Psalms* (Minneapolis: Augsburg Publishing, 1984), 68.
4. Gustavo Gutierrez, *On Job* (Maryknoll, NY: Orbis Books, 1975), 102. Ayacucho (originally, Huamanga) had been the epicenter of conflict for a number of gruesome battles both before and after *On Job*'s publication.
5. Richard C. Edgley, "Enduring Together," *Ensign*, November 2007.
6. James E. Faulconer, *Mosiah, A Brief Theological Introduction* (Provo, UT: Neal A. Maxwell Institute, 2020), 71.
7. Jeremiah Unterman, *Justice for All, How the Jewish Bible Revolutionized Ethics* (Philadelphia: Jewish Publication Society, 2017), 41–84.
8. See Martin Luther King Jr., "I Have a Dream," August 28, 1973. Full text available at https://www.npr.org/2010/01/18/122701268/i-have-a-dream-speech-in-its-entirety.
9. Walter Brueggemann, *The Message of the Psalms*, 57.
10. Chieko Okazaki, "Cat's Cradle of Kindness," *Ensign*, May 1993.
11. Walter Brueggemann, *The Message of the Psalms*, 87.
12. Denise Dombkowski Hopkins, *Journey Through the Psalms, Revised and Expanded* (St. Louis: Chalice Press, 2002), 113. Quoting Dorothee Soelle, *Suffering* (Philadelphia: Fortress Press, 1975), 70, 76.
13. Arthur Green, *Seek My Face, A Jewish Mystical Theology* (Northvale, NJ: Jewish Lights Publishing, 2012), 152.
14. Soong-Chan Rah, *Prophetic Lament, A Call for Justice in Troubled Times* (Downers Grove, IL: IVP Books, 2015), 205. While used more generally by me to demonstrate that lament moves us to action, the author is applying principles of lament to the deaths of Rodney King, Trayvon Martin, Michael Brown, Eric Garner, Tamir Rice, and others on the "long list of black victims of violence." Sadly, to that list we must also now add those like Sandra Bland, Breonna Taylor, and George Floyd.
15. M. Russell Ballard, "Doctrine of Inclusion," *Ensign*, November 2001.

A BRIEF DIVERSION ON WHAT LAMENT MIGHT LOOK LIKE

1. Dieter F. Uchtdorf, "Receiving a Testimony of Light and Truth," *Ensign*, November 2014.
2. Michael Card's book includes a section called "Journaling/Writing Your Own Lament" that might be of interest to some. See *A Sacred Sorrow: Reaching Out to God in the Lost Language of Lament* (Colorado Springs, CO: NavPress, 2005), 151–52.

NOTES

3. Page T. Johnson, "Historic conference in Washington, D.C., discusses the 'legacy of black LDS pioneers,'" *Deseret News,* February 21, 2018, https://www.thechurchnews.com/2018/2/21/23213531/historic-conference-in-washington-d-c-discusses-the-legacy-of-black-lds-pioneers.

INTERLUDE

1. "Theodicy" is a response to "the problem of evil;" I am only making a few introductory remarks here, but for a detailed survey of these issues see Michael Tooley, "The Problem of Evil," *The Stanford Encyclopedia of Philosophy* (winter 2021 edition), Edward N. Zalta, ed., https://plato.stanford.edu/archives/win2021/entries/evil/.
2. Walter Brueggemann, *The Message of the Psalms* (Minneapolis: Augsburg Publishing, 1984), 169.
3. Dale G. Renlund, "Infuriating Unfairness," *Liahona,* May 2021.
4. Quentin L. Cook, "The Songs They Could Not Sing," *Ensign,* November 2011.
5. The literature on this topic is broad. For a helpful introduction, see C. S. Lewis, *The Problem of Pain* (New York: HarperOne, 1996). For a discussion of this challenge within the context of Joseph Smith's teaching, see David L. Paulsen, "Joseph Smith and the Problem of Evil," *BYU Studies Quarterly* 39:1 (2000), Article 4, available at http://scholarsarchive.byu.edu/byusq/vol39/iss1/.
6. Walter Brueggemann, *The Message of the Psalms,* 173.
7. Amy-Jill Levine and Marc Zvi Brettler, *The Bible With and Without Jesus* (New York: HarperOne, 2020), 363.
8. Though we know that Job's original children die and that he has more children at the conclusion of the story, there is some ambiguity surrounding what becomes of Job's wife. She is only mentioned, fleetingly, at the beginning of the story and then never mentioned again. Whether she dies or not, and whether she is the mother of the second set of children, is simply not stated in the text.

CHAPTER 7

1. Different sections of scripture suggest that the Israelites were in Egypt for different lengths of time: Genesis 15:13 and Acts 7:6 suggest 400 years; however, Exodus 12:40–41 and Galatians 3:16–17 say it was 430 years. In the end, the number of years is probably irrelevant. It was a long time—that's the point. And it was long enough that the freedom of the promised land was a distant memory.
2. Brian M. Britt, "The Exodus Tradition in the Bible," n.p. [cited 13 Jan. 2022], https://www.bibleodyssey.org:443/en/passages/related-articles/exodus-tradition-in-the-bible.
3. See Claus Westermann, "The Role of the Lament in the Theology of the Old Testament," *Interpretation* 28 (1974), 20–38. Though Westermann is applying this framework to the Old Testament texts, it works equally in other scriptural contexts.
4. Walter Brueggemann, *The Message of the Psalms* (Minneapolis: Augsburg Publishing, 1984), 97.
5. As Brueggemann observes, "The sequence of *complaint-praise* is a necessary and legitimate way with God, each part in its own appropriate time. . . . One moment is not less faithful than the other." See Walter Brueggemann, *The Message of the Psalms,* 56.

NOTES

6. M. David Huston, "A Restoration of All Things?" *Public Square Magazine*, June 23, 2021.
7. Sue Monk Kidd, *When the Heart Waits: Spiritual Direction for Life's Sacred Questions* (New York: HarperOne, 1990), 27.
8. The Gospel of John has Jesus's death occurring on the day before Passover—on the Day of Preparation—when, as part of the preparation for the Passover feast, lambs would have been killed. This, theologically, makes the point that Jesus is the "Lamb of God." John also has the Passover and Sabbath occurring on the same day (Saturday), whereas the synoptics have Passover occurring on Friday (the day before the Sabbath). These differences, while interesting theologically, do not alter the fact highlighted herein: that the time of waiting between death and resurrection was the longest part of the death/resurrection process.
9. Jeffrey R. Holland, "The First Great Commandment," *Ensign*, November 2012.
10. Deidre Nicole Green, *Jacob, A Brief Theological Introduction* (Provo, UT: Neal A. Maxwell Institute, 2020), 24.
11. Shelly Rambo, *Spirit and Trauma, A Theology of Remaining* (Louisville, KY: Westminster Press, 2010).
12. Deidre Nicole Green, *Jacob, A Brief Theological Introduction*, 25.
13. Deidre Nicole Green, *Jacob, A Brief Theological Introduction*, 26.
14. Joseph B. Wirthlin, "Sunday Will Come," *Ensign*, November 2006.
15. Barbara Brown Taylor, *Learning to Walk in the Dark* (New York: Harper Collins, 2014), 77–78.
16. Jeffrey R. Holland, "Waiting on the Lord," *Ensign*, November 2020.
17. Sue Monk Kidd, *When the Heart Waits*, 26.
18. Henry B. Eyring, "Waiting upon the Lord," Brigham Young University devotional address, September 30, 1990.
19. Robert D. Hales, "Waiting upon the Lord: Thy Will Be Done," *Ensign*, November 2011.
20. Walter Brueggemann explains, "Faith does not always resolve life. . . . Too much pastoral action is inclined and tempted to resolve things, no matter how the situation really is. Faith is treated like the great answer book. Insofar as these [laments] are witnesses to faith, they attest that *faith means staying in the midst of the disorientation*, not retreating to an old orientation that is over and done with, and not charging ahead to some imagined resolution that rushes ahead of the slow, tortuous pace of reality" (*The Message of the Psalms*, 78; emphasis added).
21. Thomas S. Monson, "Finding Joy in the Journey," *Ensign*, November 2008.
22. Walter Brueggemann, *The Message of the Psalms*, 59.
23. Vilate Raile, "Upon the Cross of Calvary," *Hymns* (1985), no. 184.
24. The male-centeredness of the text is not lost on me, but such is the nature of biblical text sometimes.
25. See Walter Brueggemann, *The Message of the Psalms*, 77. Though he was speaking of Psalm 137, Walter Brueggemann's point seems to apply to Jeremiah as well: "The capacity to leave vengeance to God may free Israel [or Jeremiah] for its primary vocation, which is the tenacious hope that prevents sell-out. Indeed, one may speculate

NOTES

that if Israel [or Jeremiah] could not boldly leave vengeance to God and had worried about vengeance on its own, Israel [or Jeremiah] might have had no energy or freedom to hope. Perhaps it is precisely the capacity to turn that over to God which leaves Israel [or Jeremiah] free to hope."

26. Robert D. Hales, "Your Sorrow Shall Be Turned to Joy," *Ensign*, November 1983.
27. Joseph B. Wirthlin, "Sunday Will Come," *Ensign*, November 2006; emphasis added.
28. See Dale G. Renlund, "Consider the Goodness and Greatness of God," *Ensign*, May 2020.
29. The Hebrew text also suggests, potentially, one "selling one's self," e.g., to settle a debt.
30. Neal A. Maxwell, "Hope through the Atonement of Jesus Christ," *Ensign,* November 1998.
31. Sue Monk Kidd, *When the Heart Waits*, Pg. 26.
32. Shelly Rambo expresses this idea beautifully. She explains: "There is no life after the storm but only life reconceived by the storm." See Shelly Rambo, *Spirit and Trauma, A Theology of Remaining* (Westminster Press: Louisville, KY, 2010), 109.
33. Walter Brueggemann, *Praying the Psalms* (Cascade Books: Eugene, OR, 2007), 22.
34. Walter Brueggemann observes of ancient Israel's sacred tradition, "The remarkable thing about Israel is that it did not banish or deny the darkness from its religious enterprise. It embraces the darkness as the very stuff of new life. Indeed, Israel seems to know that new life comes from nowhere else" (*The Message of the Psalms*, 53).
35. Dieter F. Uchtdorf, "Daily Restoration," *Liahona*, November 2021.
36. M. David Huston, "A Restoration of All Things?"
37. Neal A. Maxwell, "Consecrate Thy Performance," *Ensign*, May 2002.
38. Barbara Brown Taylor, *Holy Envy* (New York: HarperOne, 2019), 156.
39. Soong-Chan Rah, *Prophetic Lament, A Call for Justice in Troubled Times* (Downers Grove, IL: IVP Books, 2015), 203.
40. Abraham Joshua Heschel, *God in Search of Man* (FSG Books: NY, 1976), 238.

EPILOGUE

1. "Elder and Sister Holland Share a New Year's Message of Hope in Christ," The Church of Jesus Christ of Latter-day Saints, *Newsroom*, January 8, 2023.
2. As President Dieter F. Uchtdorf said, "In nearly 200 years of Church history—along with an uninterrupted line of inspired, honorable, and divine events—there have been some things said and done that could cause people to question" ("Come, Join with Us," *Ensign*, November 2013).
3. It is too easy to dismiss those who leave the Latter-day Saint community as unfaithful or uncommitted. In my experience knowing many people who *have* left, the reasons are far, far more complex than we are sometimes willing to acknowledge.
4. Barbara Brown Taylor, *When God Is Silent* (Norwich, England: Canterbury Press, 2013), 118.
5. Michael Card, *A Sacred Sorrow: Reaching Out to God in the Lost Language of Lament* (Colorado Springs, CO: NavPress, 2005), 129.

BIBLIOGRAPHY

Allen, Wayne. *Thinking about Good and Evil, Jewish Views from Antiquity to Modernity*. Philadelphia: Jewish Publication Society, 2021.
Bail, Ulrike. "O God Hear My Prayer: Psalm 55 and Violence against Women." In *Wisdom and Psalms: A Feminist Companion to the Bible* (2nd series), edited by Athalya Brenner and Carole Fontaine. Sheffield, England: Sheffield Academic Press, 1998.
Ballard, M. Russell. "Doctrine of Inclusion." *Ensign*, November 2001.
Belnap, Daniel. "A Comparison of the Communal Lament Psalms and the Treaty-Covenant Formula." *Studies in the Bible and Antiquity*, vol. 1, 2009.
Berlin, Adele and Marc Zvi Brettler, ed. *The Jewish Study Bible, 2nd edition*. New York: Oxford University Press, 2014.
Bowler, Kate. *Everything Happens for a Reason and Other Lies I've Loved*. New York: Random House, 2019.
Britt, Brian M. "Exodus Tradition in the Bible." Accessed January 13, 2022. https://www.bibleodyssey.org:443/en/passages/related-articles/exodus-tradition-in-the-bible.
Brueggemann, Walter, "The Costly Loss of Lament." In Patrick D. Miller, ed., *The Psalms and the Life of Faith*. Minneapolis: Fortress Press, 1995.
Brueggemann, Walter. *The Message of the Psalms*. Minneapolis: Augsburg Publishing, 1984.
Brueggemann, Walter. *Praying the Psalms*. Eugene, OR: Cascade Books, 2007.
Card, Michael. *A Sacred Sorrow: Reaching Out to God in the Lost Language of Lament*. Colorado Springs, CO: NavPress, 2005.
Centers for Disease Control and Prevention, National Center for Health Statistics. "Anxiety and Depression, Household Pulse Survey." https://www.cdc.gov/nchs/covid19/pulse/mental-health.htm.
Christofferson, D. Todd. "Our Relationship with God." *Liahona*, May 2022.
Christofferson, D. Todd. "Why the Church." *Ensign*, November 2015.
Come, Follow Me—For Individuals and Families: Old Testament 2022. Salt Lake City: The Church of Jesus Christ of Latter-day Saints, 2021.
Cook, Quentin L. "The Songs They Could Not Sing." *Ensign*, November 2011.
Cornish, J. Devn. "The Privilege of Prayer." *Ensign*, November 2011.
Davies, Dean M. "The Blessings of Worship." *Ensign*, November 2016.

BIBLIOGRAPHY

"Doctrine and Covenants, 1844," p. 69, The Joseph Smith Papers. Accessed January 5, 2022. https://www.josephsmithpapers.org/paper-summary/doctrine-and-covenants-1844/71.

Edgley, Richard C. "Enduring Together." *Ensign*, November 2007.

"Elder and Sister Holland Share a New Year's Message of Hope in Christ." The Church Newsroom, January 8, 2023.

Eyring, Henry B. "Waiting upon the Lord." Brigham Young University devotional address, September 30, 1990.

Faulconer, James E. *Mosiah, A Brief Theological Introduction*. Provo, UT: Neal A. Maxwell Institute, 2020.

Gibson, Rachel Sterzer. "Latter-day Saint youth and suicide: What to know and how to help." *Church News*, September 2, 2021.

Givens, Fiona and Terryl. *The Christ Who Heals: How God Restored the Truth That Saves Us*. Salt Lake City: Deseret Book, 2017.

Givens, Terryl. *Wrestling the Angel*. England: Oxford University Press, 2015.

Goldman, William. *The Princess Bride, 30th Anniversary Edition*. New York: Random House, 2003.

Green, Arthur. *Seek My Face, A Jewish Mystical Theology*. Northvale, NJ: Jewish Lights Publishing, 2012.

Green, Deidre Nicole. *Jacob, A Brief Theological Introduction*. Provo, UT: Neal A. Maxwell Institute, 2020.

Gunkel, Hermann. *Introduction to the Psalm: The Genres of Religious Lyric of Israel*, trans. James D. Nogalski. Macon, GA: Mercer Press, 1998.

Gutierrez, Gustavo. *On Job*. Maryknoll, NY: Orbis Books, 1970.

Hackett, Jo Ann. "1 and 2 Samuel." In Carol A. Newsom, et al., ed. *Women's Bible Commentary, 20th Anniversary Edition*. Louisville, KY: Westminster Press, 2012.

Hales, Robert D. "Waiting upon the Lord: Thy Will Be Done," *Ensign*, November 2011.

Hales, Robert D. "Your Sorrow Shall Be Turned to Joy," *Ensign*, November 1983.

Heschel, Abraham Joshua. *God in Search of Man*. New York: FSG Books, 1976.

Hilton III, John. "Old Testament Psalms in the Book of Mormon." In Jeffrey R. Chadwick, Matthew J. Grey, and David Rolph Seely, ed. *Ascending the Mountain of the Lord: Temple, Praise, and Worship in the Old Testament* (2013 Sperry Symposium). Provo, UT: Religious Studies Center, Brigham Young University, 2013.

"History, 1838–1856, volume D-1 [1 August 1842–1 July 1843] [addenda]," p. 3 [addenda], The Joseph Smith Papers. Accessed December 22, 2021. https://www.josephsmithpapers.org/paper-summary/history-1838–1856-volume-d-1–1-august-1842–1-july-1843/284.

Holland, Jeffrey R. "The First Great Commandment." *Ensign*, November 2012.

Holland, Jeffrey R. "Like a Broken Vessel." *Ensign*, November 2013.

Holland, Jeffrey R. "Look to God and Live." *Ensign*, November 1993.

Holland, Jeffrey R. "None Were with Him." *Ensign*, May 2009.

Holland, Jeffrey R. "Waiting on the Lord." *Ensign*, November 2020.

Hopkins, Denise Dombkowski. *Journey Through the Psalms, Revised and Expanded*. St. Louis: Chalice Press, 2002.

BIBLIOGRAPHY

Huston, M. David. "A Restoration of All Things?" *Public Square Magazine*, June 23, 2021.

Johnson, Jane Clayson. *Silent Souls Weeping*. Salt Lake City: Deseret Book, 2018.

Johnson, Page T., "Historic conference in Washington, D.C., discusses the 'legacy of black LDS pioneers'" *Deseret News*, February 21, 2018.

Kidd, Sue Monk. *When the Heart Waits: Spiritual Direction for Life's Sacred Questions*. New York: HarperOne, 1990.

King, Jr., Martin Luther, "I Have a Dream," August 28, 1973. https://www.npr.org/2010/01/18/122701268/i-have-a-dream-speech-in-its-entirety.

Lewis, C. S. *The Problem of Pain*. New York: HarperOne, 1996.

"Losing 25,000 to Hunger Every Day." *The UN Chronicle*. Accessed January 8, 2022. https://www.un.org/en/chronicle/article/losing-25000-hunger-every-day.

Monson, Thomas S. "Finding Joy in the Journey." *Ensign*, November 2008.

Maxwell, Neal A. "Apply the Atoning Blood of Christ." *Ensign*, November 1997.

Maxwell, Neal A. "Consecrate Thy Performance." *Ensign*, May 2002.

Maxwell, Neal A. "Hope through the Atonement of Jesus Christ." *Ensign*, November 1998.

Maxwell, Neal A. "Murmur Not." *Ensign*, November 1989.

Nelson, Russell M. "Joy and Spiritual Survival." *Ensign*, November 2016.

Nelson, Russell M. "Revelation for the Church, Revelation for our Lives," *Ensign*, May 2018.

Newman, John Henry. "The Pillar and the Cloud." In *Lead, Kindly Light: Meditations, Poems, and Prayers for the Journey*, vol. 1. Acropolis Scholars, 2019.

Okazaki, Chieko. "Cat's Cradle of Kindness," *Ensign*, May 1993.

Paulsen, David L. "Joseph Smith and the Problem of Evil." *BYU Studies Quarterly* 39:1.

"People and Poverty." *The World Counts* (website). Accessed January 8, 2022. https://www.theworldcounts.com/challenges/people-and-poverty/hunger-and-obesity/how-many-people-die-from-hunger-each-year/story;

Pew Research Center. "Religion's Relationship to Happiness, Civic Engagement and Health around the World." January 31, 2019.

Pew Research Center. "Religious Landscape Study." 2014.

Rah, Soong-Chan. *Prophetic Lament: A Call for Justice in Troubled Times*. Downers Grove, IL: IVP Books, 2015.

Rambo, Shelly. *Spirit and Trauma: A Theology of Remaining*. Louisville, KY: Westminster Press, 2010.

Renlund, Dale G. "Consider the Goodness and Greatness of God." *Ensign*, May 2020.

Renlund, Dale G. "Infuriating Unfairness." *Liahona*, May 2021.

The Rule of St. Benedict. Carolinne White, trans. London: Penguin Classics, 2008.

Sharecare. "Community Well-Being Index." Accessed December 2, 2021. https://wellbeingindex.sharecare.com/.

Soelle, Dorothy. *Suffering*. Philadelphia: Fortress Press, 1975.

Taylor, Barbara Brown. *Holy Envy*. New York: HarperOne, 2019.

Taylor, Barbara Brown. *Learning to Walk in the Dark*. New York: Harper Collins, 2014.

Taylor, Barbara Brown. *When God Is Silent*. Norwich, England: Canterbury Press, 2013.

BIBLIOGRAPHY

Teachings of Presidents of the Church: Gordon B. Hinckley. Salt Lake City: The Church of Jesus Christ of Latter-day Saints, 2016.

Tooley, Michael. "The Problem of Evil." *The Stanford Encyclopedia of Philosophy*, Winter 2021.

Uchtdorf, Dieter F. "Come Join with Us." *Ensign*, November 2013.

Uchtdorf, Dieter F. "Daily Restoration." *Liahona*, November 2021.

Uchtdorf, Dieter F. "Receiving a Testimony of Light and Truth." *Liahona*, November 2014.

Unterman, Jeremiah. *Justice for All, How the Jewish Bible Revolutionized Ethics.* Philadelphia: Jewish Publication Society, 2017.

"Visiting Teaching Message: Participate in Sincere Prayer." *Liahona*, June 2009.

Westerman, Claus. *The Psalms: Structure, Content, and Message.* Ralph D. Gehrke, trans. Minneapolis: Augsburg Publishing House, 1980.

Westermann, Claus. "The Role of the Lament in the Theology of the Old Testament." *Interpretation* 28 (1974).

Wirthlin, Joseph B. "Sunday Will Come." *Ensign*, November 2006.

ABOUT THE AUTHOR

MICHAEL HUSTON currently resides in central Maryland. He received degrees from Utah State University (Logan, UT), American University (Washington, DC), and Wesley Theological Seminary (Washington, DC). Though he spent much of his youth west of the Mississippi, he has lived on the east coast for more than twenty years. He and his wife of twenty-three years have four children.